CU00970836

Witnessing History

Looking at oral evidence

Further history titles from Stanley Thornes and Hulton include:

KELLY *A World of Change: Britain in the Early Modern Age 1450–1700*
  World of Change Topic Books:
    A City at War: Oxford 1642–46
    Elizabeth & Akbar: Portraits of Power
    Scolding Tongues: The Persecution of Witches
    Bare Ruined Choirs: The Fate of a Welsh Abbey
    Exploring other Civilisations
    Children in Tudor England
    The Cromwell Family
    To the New World: The Founding of Pennsylvania

LEEDS *Peace and War: A First Source Book*

SAUVAIN *British Economic and Social History – Book 1 1700–1890*
                                        Book 2 1850–present day

  Hulton New Histories:
    1 *Tribes and Tribunes*
    2 *Serf and Crusader*
    3 *Crown and Parliament*
    4 *Forge and Factory*
    5 *War and Peace*
    Teacher's Book

  GCSE History Companions:
    Skills for Modern World History
    Skills for British and European History
    Skills for British Economic and Social History

  Modern World History – 1919–onwards

  European and World History – 1815–1919

  Lively History
    Town and Country – 1485–1789
    Empire, City and Industry – 1789–1901
    Conflict, Science and Society: The Twentieth Century

SIMPSON *Changing Horizons: Britain 1914–1980*

  Working with Sources: Case Studies in Twentieth Century History

WHITING (Series co-ordinator) *Footprints*
  Industry
  The Countryside
  Towns
  Churches

Witnessing History

Looking at oral evidence

Stuart M. Archer

and

Nigel Shepley

Stanley Thornes (Publishers) Ltd

Text © Stuart M. Archer and Nigel Shepley 1988

All rights reserved. No part of this publication may be reproduced, stored in a retrieval system or transmitted in any form or by any means, electronic, mechanical, photocopying, recording or otherwise, without the prior written consent of the copyright holders. Applications for such permission should be addressed to the publishers: Stanley Thornes (Publishers) Ltd, Old Station Drive, Leckhampton, CHELTENHAM GL53 0DN, England.

First published in 1988 by:
Stanley Thornes (Publishers) Ltd
Old Station Drive
Leckhampton
CHELTENHAM GL53 0DN
England

British Library Cataloguing in Publication Data

Archer, Stuart
    Witnessing history.
    1. Great Britain. 1918–1940—For schools
    I. Title   II. Shepley, Nigel
    941.083

    ISBN 0-85950-828-5

Typeset by Tech-Set, Gateshead, Tyne & Wear.
Printed and bound in Great Britain at The Bath Press, Avon.

Contents

Preface: using oral evidence

With the help of Aeolus, king of the winds, Odysseus sailed to within sight of his island home of Ithaca. Aeolus had tied up all the adverse winds in a goatskin, but thinking that it contained treasure, the sailors opened it up while their captain slept. Thus they were blown away from the shore again and swept far to the west.

Peter Lowe, *Gods, Men and Monsters*, 1977

This is an extract from the ancient story of the Trojan war and the subsequent wanderings of Odysseus as he tried to return home when the war was over. The Greeks regarded such tales as part of their history. The stories of the Trojan war were handed down by word of mouth for hundreds of years until they were finally recorded in written form by the poet Homer. As time had passed, the stories were exaggerated and elaborated to make them more exciting to audiences. They do not read like history as we now know it; but historians think that there really was a Trojan war and that the myths about Aeolus and the gods which Homer and others added can help us to understand how the ancient Greeks thought and how they tried to explain the natural world.

Ever since ancient times, the memories of people about their past have been used by historians. This book presents some oral evidence to illustrate social and economic themes in British history between 1918 and 1939. We interviewed over eighty men and women about their experiences and attitudes in this period.

Oral evidence is not in itself history, but is simply a part of the raw material which can be used to write history. Like all other sources it contains gaps, inconsistencies and prejudices. A sample of less than one hundred 'witnesses' cannot claim to be entirely representative. Many of those to whom we spoke came from the north of England, where most of the interviews were conducted; fewer came from the south or from Scotland. Readers are encouraged to fill in some of the gaps by carrying out interviews themselves. The text contains questions and suggests oral history assignments, and the final section gives some advice on collecting oral evidence. The questions are arranged under three headings (Understanding, Assessment and Analysis, and Empathy) which are designed to meet the assessment criteria for GCSE examinations, although the material can be used at other stages of a school history syllabus.

Oral sources can supplement the more conventional primary evidence of government reports, Parliamentary debates, political memoirs and newspaper headlines, to give a direct line to the ideas, occupations, circumstances and beliefs of 'ordinary' people in the inter-war years.

'As any . . . historian knows, it is easier to describe the externals of a past age than to get inside the people themselves, into their thoughts and feelings.' M.I. Finley wrote these words about ancient Greece. They remain true of more recent history. For example, the conventional historical sources allow us to follow the foreign policy which took Britain to war in 1939. Neville Chamberlain, the Prime Minister, recorded on the outbreak of war:

Everything that I have worked for, everything that I have hoped for, everything that I have believed in . . . has crashed in ruins.

Oral evidence can show how the work of government affected ordinary men and women and what their reactions were. One housewife took no interest in international affairs, and remembered only how the coming of war unexpectedly interrupted her party for her wedding anniversary:

> We didn't listen to the news. I didn't know Mr Chamberlain had been to see Hitler. The war was unexpected. It began on our wedding anniversary. I was washing up all that day.

The wife of a Yorkshire greengrocer told us that her immediate concerns were for her family and her business:

> My immediate reaction was fear that my sons might have to go and fight. When the war broke out it meant that our expectations of a good Christmas display at our new shop were disappointed – we had planned for it all year.
>
> When rationing came, people we had never seen before pretended to be old and loyal customers; we had sleepless nights in 1940, not because of air raids, but because rabbits were scarce, and we had to share out a few among many.
>
> One man complained that he was half an ounce short in his ration of oranges. People who had once seemed to be carefree became greedy, disgruntled and ridiculous.

Listening to and analysing the memories of those who lived through this recent period is a vital way of probing their mentality, their states of mind, of getting 'inside the people themselves'. The historian cannot afford to ignore the spoken word.

Stuart M. Archer
Nigel Shepley
1988

Acknowledgements

The authors and publishers are grateful to the following for permission to reproduce previously published material:

Oxford University Press for extracts from *A Survey of the Social Structure of England and Wales* by A.M. Carr-Saunders and D. Caradog Jones, 2nd edn, 1937.

We would also like to thank the following for providing photographs and illustrations and permission to reproduce them:

BBC Hulton Picture Library (pp. 3, 6, 34, 38, 43, 47, 54, 56, 64, 65, 66, 67, 72, 73, 74, 75, 77, 88, 90)

British Coal (pp. 46, 49)

Greater London Record Office (p. 25)

Imperial War Museum (p. 4)

Keystone (pp. 78, 80)

Mansell Collection (p. 11)

National Railway Museum (p. 92)

Popperfoto (pp. 18, 36, 51)

Pyms Gallery (p. 71)

Marie Stopes clinic (p. 9)

Wolfgang Suschitzky (pp. 16, 29)

1 Aftermath of War

A group of Yorkshire soldiers, 1918

On 11 November 1918, Germany signed an armistice which ended four years of fighting in the 'Great War'.

Nearly three-quarters of a million men from the United Kingdom had been killed (9 per cent of all those aged between 20 and 45). One million and seven hundred thousand were wounded. David Lloyd George, the British Prime Minister, was horrified that 'Europe had been drenched with the blood of its bravest and best', but hoped that this had been 'the war to end all wars'.

Soon schools, churches, villages, towns and cities began to erect monuments and plaques, listing the local dead. Few families escaped

mourning for 'the lost generation'. For almost all, the war was a turning point.

Mixed with the bitterness and grief there was a determination that the sacrifice and waste would lead to positive gain. Good must be made to come from such appalling evil. Lloyd George coined the catch-phrase, promising 'a land fit for heroes'.

Hopes were raised. If millions of pounds a day could be spent in war, why could not millions be spent in peace to provide 'reconstruction' – a better society which would care for the old, the sick, the poor and the young? Why not build houses, hospitals and schools, rather than guns, tanks and battleships?

SOURCE 1
Memories of a Yorkshire businessman who fought in the war

I was in the Army in France, in charge of a wireless station. We were advancing. We knew things were happening. We were in the forest of Valenciennes. I set up a wireless station in a farm house which had been occupied by the Germans for four years. I was made very comfortable – in fact, the daughter wanted to court me.

I was in the habit of taking the news every night at ten o' clock, and taking it to the Colonel every morning. On November 10th I was listening in. The farmer's wife was in the kitchen, making Yorkshire puddings. I took the news down in French, which showed us that the armistice was on its way. I sat up all night. Hostilities were to end at 11 a.m. next morning. At seven I gave the message to the Colonel. We were all delighted, but not as delighted as the civilians. First of all, we didn't believe it, and second of all we were in the middle of a bloody wood!

We got dressed in farm clothes (me and another soldier). I wore the wife's. We went into the village, had some drinks and went back. We weren't supposed to be in civilian clothes, but we walked straight past the Colonel and he never said anything. Guns were still firing at one o' clock – most of them didn't know the news.

I was only twenty when the war ended. I'd run away from grammar school to join the army. I'd been Captain of the school at football and cricket. I was a young, volunteer, athletic recruit. I couldn't see the seriousness of life; I still couldn't when I came out. I could have gone to university if I'd wanted to, but I went into business instead, marrying the boss's daughter (which is the best way, you know).

I was never brought up as a toff. I could mix with officers, but I wouldn't be one. I ran off to look smart. We were getting white feathers every day.

SOURCE 2
A retired RAF officer who was a schoolboy in London

I was at school on that day, and someone rushed into the classroom and said, 'The war's over'. Pandemonium reigned. They dismissed the school. We rushed home. Police in vans with loud hailers disseminated the news. Newspapers published special editions. Immediately there were cries of 'Hang the Kaiser!' It was going to be a land fit for heroes to live in.

For years and years armistice day was very, very serious. Anyone who did not stop and remove his hat at 11 o' clock was likely to be publicly assaulted.

SOURCE 3
A Durham miner who had been badly wounded in the war

I remember Lloyd George promising 'a land fit for heroes'. I said at the time, 'It won't be fit to die in'.

SOURCE 4

Ex-servicemen in a London street, 1918

SOURCE 5

Extract from an address by a headmistress to Edinburgh schoolgirls in 1917 (from a report in a school magazine)

Sweets are an unnecessary extravagance. Any unnecessary use of sugar is nothing short of unpatriotic. . . . Rigid economy is particularly the woman's task and a personal one. The habit of spending must be stopped at all costs because, though we have the money, we have not the food. . . . The kitchen holds the key to victory.

SOURCE 6

Extract from a letter from a Scottish nurse in Serbia

The wounded were lying on sacks of straw on the floor, and everything was horribly dirty. We had the wards whitewashed and got our beds put up, and things are looking very nice. The men are charming and tremendously brave. . . . One poor man died the other day. The other patients asked leave to sing their National Anthem while he had his last cup of coffee. I am awfully happy working out here.

SOURCE 7
*Munitions girls
– For King and
Country by
E.F. Skinner*

Questions

UNDERSTANDING

1. In Source 1 explain 'We were getting white feathers every day.'

2. What evidence is there in Source 1 that the news of peace led to a relaxing of military discipline?

3. In Source 2 who was the Kaiser?

4. In Source 5 what does the phrase 'rigid economy' mean? How does the headmistress believe that schoolgirls and women can help the war effort?

5. 'Things are looking very nice' (Source 6). What improvements had the nurses made?

6. How are the girls in Source 7 helping the war effort?

ASSESSMENT AND ANALYSIS

1. In Source 1 what evidence is there that the British soldier got on well with French civilians?

2. What evidence is there of bitterness against Germany in Source 2?

3.
   SINKINGS OF BRITISH SHIPS BY ENEMY SUBMARINES

   Jan. 1918 – 57
   Feb. 1918 – 68
   Mar. 1918 – 79

   What connection would you make between these figures and Source 5?

4. If you were studying the First World War, what kinds of people would you try to interview in order to ensure that there were as few gaps in your evidence as possible?

EMPATHY

1. Read Source 1 again. Describe the motives of a schoolboy in joining the Army.

2. 'Anyone who did not stop and remove his hat at 11 o' clock was likely to be publicly assaulted' (Source 2). Can you explain why this was so?

3. 'A land fit for heroes' (Source 3). Why do you think Lloyd George made this promise during the 1918 election? What do you think the ex-servicemen in Source 4 (with their records of war service and pictures of their wives and children) thought about Lloyd George's promise?

4. Can you explain why the young nurse in Source 6 felt 'awfully happy'?

2 The People of Britain
from the cradle to the grave

Between 1918 and 1939 the population of Great Britain continued to grow, but much more slowly than in the nineteenth century. Both the birth and death rates were falling, and the number of older people was increasing. The expectation of life had risen steadily in the past 50 years, until in 1938 it reached almost 62 years for men and almost 66 years for women.

Improved social conditions also led to a decrease in the number of babies dying before they reached their first birthday. The infant mortality rate fell from 110 per 1000 in the years before 1914 to 57 per 1000 in 1935, but this national figure does not show the alarming differences between regions and social classes. One important reason for the fall in the deaths of babies may well have been the trend towards smaller family size. The spread of birth control through the ideas of pioneers such as Dr Marie Stopes encouraged the working classes to limit the size of their families.

The chances of survival of their babies, the schools to which they would go, their future jobs, pay, houses, hospitals, holidays, savings and pensions – these were the main concerns of the people of Britain.

Central and local government had long been involved in attempts to improve social conditions, but between the wars the range of social services was by no means complete or comprehensive. Improvements were made, particularly in housing, but serious gaps still existed. Insurance against unemployment was not universal. Family allowances were not provided. There was no national health service: in 1936 only half the population was covered by insurance against sickness. Doctors still charged for their care and their medicines, calling weekly at the houses of their patients to collect their bills in instalments.

C.L. Mowat wrote that 'the Welfare State was standing, but still incomplete and in scaffolding. . . . Not until after 1945 were the gaps filled, the walls finished, and a roof put over all.'

BIRTH

SOURCE 1

A Yorkshire miner's wife

I bought all the baby clothes new at first. Her grandma bought one new thing each week. They were good stuff, but cheap. I made them do for my son, ten years later.

I got a new pram. It was only £4, in a little sweet shop at the bottom of the road – we paid 2s. 6d. a week. There were no baby shops then like now. I sold that pram for 4s. one Thursday so I could buy some tea – pay day was Friday and I had run short of money.

I had my daughter before the 1939 war. At the maternity home we had to pay £2 deposit and another 10s. when she came. I got up at six o' clock in the morning and said to my husband, 'Come on, we're ready'. I had to walk down to the maternity home with a hole in my shoe. The night before that I'd black-leaded the fireplace.

I never went to the doctor's. There was a post-natal clinic, but I didn't go. I went when I had my second child during the Second World War, because you could get free orange juice then. We had no dried milk. I breast fed them. We couldn't afford to buy milk. Most people couldn't. We got no help at all with anything. Only the doctor's wife had a nanny round here.

Mother and baby in the early 1930s

SOURCE 2
Advertisement for 'Trufood' (Punch, August 1936)

TRUFOOD BABIES
become sturdy children

Another Trufood baby—this lovely little girl is the daughter of Lady Ankaret Jackson.

You see the results of correct infant-feeding when a Trufood baby begins to sit erect and to crawl. The straight back, the firm energetic little body and the sturdy limbs speak of the perfectly-balanced nourishment that the little one has been receiving. Humanised Trufood feeds every cell of Baby's body and brain just as perfect breast milk does. Every characteristic of breast milk is reproduced in Humanised Trufood.

POST THIS COUPON
"CRADLE DAYS"
Our booklet " CRADLE DAYS " is a guide for Mothers on the care and well-being of Baby. May we send you a free copy, together with a sample of Humanised Trufood? Post the coupon to Trufood Limited, Dept. PUN 86, The Creameries, Wrenbury, Cheshire. *(Samples duty free I.F.S.)*

NAME ....

ADDRESS ....

....

SOURCE 3
A Scottish doctor

In my student days we had a lecture by the famous Marie Stopes on birth control. It was a very lively lecture. The women students were dead against her. She pioneered birth control, and she was on the right lines, completely. She argued that birth control would lead to better health for mothers and therefore better health for the baby.

Infant mortality was bound to be higher in large families. The mother had far more children to look after, and to cope with on the living wage of the husband. Big families were still fairly common. When I was a student at Manchester, I went out with the midwives to study my midwifery, and it was not uncommon to go into a house either in the working class part of Manchester, or to the dockland at Salford, to find a mother about to have her twelfth or fourteenth child.

The huge size of families was quite unnecessary, and was just evidence of lack of self-control. Birth control was beginning to emerge, but it took a long time.

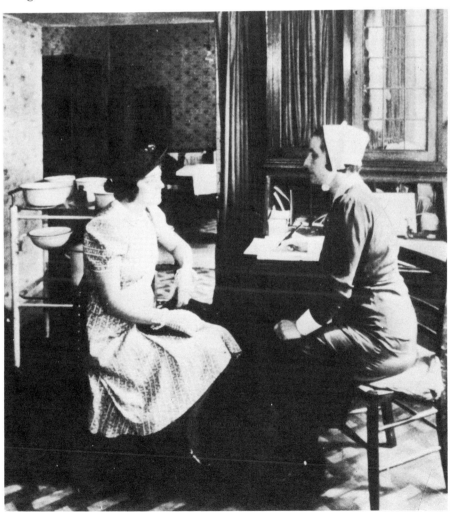

The Marie Stopes Clinic

DISEASES AND DOCTORS

SOURCE 4

A Nottinghamshire furniture salesman's childhood memories

Some families' children were wiped out with diptheria. We were plagued with all sorts of killer diseases – diptheria, whooping cough, scarlet fever, tuberculosis. At school, during epidemics, we gargled with potassium permanganate. Some children used to have impetigo: they used to put purple stuff on their faces, and you kept as far away from them as you could.

impetigo = a very infectious skin disease

SOURCE 5

A schoolboy from Yorkshire, later a hospital porter

At thirteen years old I went into hospital for twenty-six weeks, when I was put in an iron lung. The doctors and nurses were really kind. The food was marvellous compared to what I had been used to getting. They had a pool for sweets and you all got an equal share.

SOURCE 6

A retired soldier from London who served in India

I had malaria five times. There were three sorts – one eats the body, one the liver, one the brain. I got the body type. I was fed on raw liver.

You could get cholera in the villages. There was plenty of rabies about, and mad dogs. I once got bitten by a dog. Next day I went to the old quack. They asked me for two rupees to take the dog to the vet for tests – it had died after it bit me. I had to have injections. Dogs would jump into prams and bite babies.

SOURCE 7

A shopkeeper in a Yorkshire mining village who was at school in the 1930s

Doctors were very hard worked then. Round here they were retained by the colliery. If a fellow was off for a week he had to go for a special examination. They pulled teeth out with no anaesthetic. They went round on bikes. Good doctors they were – no tackle, no special knowledge, but good. I remember my father taking me to the doctor to have a tooth out. I ran under the table. They had to pull me out before they could pull the tooth. The doctor took Woodbines in payment. Medicine was just too dear.

SOURCE 8

A London housewife

I had a brain tumour removed when I was 22. In a private hospital. My name was in all the journals.

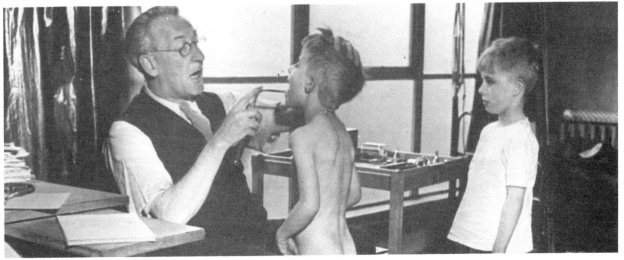

The school health services developed rapidly in the inter-war years

SOURCE 9

A Scottish doctor (See also Source 3)

I started in general practice in West Lothian. In the country districts we had three small hamlets to look after – collections of miners' dwellings. At least two of these villages – only seventeen miles from Edinburgh – still had dry closets. When I went on my rounds on a morning I would see the night soil man going round with his horse and cart. They had no electric lighting in these cottages; it was all candles and oil lamps. One delivered mothers and attended children in these conditions.

I'm not criticising the family doctors – after all, I was one in the 1920s. But the opening of infant welfare clinics meant that the mother could get medical advice without payment. Otherwise she would have had to go to the private doctor and pay. We attended several working class people in Scotland. They were very nice folk indeed and they scraped and saved so that they could always pay the doctor when he called.

The impact of the new drugs began just before the Second World War. In the City Fever Hospital in Newcastle in 1938 I treated my first patient with some stuff called 'Prontosil'. It was the forerunner of all the sulphonamides. The result was quite dramatic. These drugs revolutionised the treatment of mothers and children. And now we have a whole range of drugs.

When I was working with my brother in Scotland we had a whooping cough outbreak. We knew that no matter what we prescribed and no matter what we did we were likely to lose at least one child. There was no specific remedy as we have it today with modern penicillins.

DEATH

SOURCE 10
*The wife of an
Air Force officer
in London*

Father's funeral was very sad. He'd never been ill before. He came home at eleven in the morning and said, 'This is the end of me, mother.' He'd got pneumonia. The nurse said, 'Don't worry, we have new drugs, we can treat pneumonia now.' But he seemed to get worse and worse. He was in a room, very cold, with all the windows open and a grey pneumonia jacket on. He was 58. I don't feel he got the best treatment.

SOURCE 11
*A mill worker
and Labour
Councillor
in Yorkshire*

Funerals in the 1930s were really something. Now you rush through them as quickly as possible. Death was accepted. In the old days, the parson would talk for twenty minutes about the dead person; today you get him out of the way and forget all about him. There was always a meal at a funeral. There was concern for the individual, felt for a person as a person.

SOURCE 12
*A solicitor's
wife in the north
of England*

Grandfather's funeral was a terrific gathering of the clans. Everyone wore black from head to foot. The whole family went into mourning in a real way. Mother was mourning for five or six months.

SOURCE 13
*A school
caretaker in
west Yorkshire*

My earliest memory is of my dad lifting me up to look at my mother in her coffin. She died with her baby of dropsy in the workhouse. We couldn't afford to send her anywhere else.

A Poor Law funeral was a terrible disgrace. It happened to people who died in the workhouse – they were put in a box and dumped.

SOURCE 14
*A London
housewife*

Death was more talked about. Among the old there was a much stronger belief in life after death. My mother believed in life after death, just like that. What God has in store for us, I am much less certain of than she was.

SOURCE 15

A parish priest in the Midlands

There's no question of the impact of the slaughter in France in World War One. Even people who didn't go to church used to have a general belief in Christianity. But the Great War was a tremendous test of people's faith.

People had got fed up with discipline and being bossed around, and church going. They were a tired generation, and they didn't want any more of it. And who can blame them, really?

Today you have two generations of people who have less Christian upbringing than before. The mass deaths of 1914–18 and the Blitz deaths of 1940 made people feel life was a much less secure thing. On the whole people still expect a good funeral, but perhaps with not much religion in it.

Questions

UNDERSTANDING

1. What makes you think that the miner's wife (Source 1) was poor?

2. Why was infant mortality likely to be higher in large families (Source 3)?

3. Make a list of all the illnesses mentioned in Sources 4 to 9. Which of these were common in the 1920s and 1930s but are now rare?

4. Find evidence in Sources 4 to 9 to show that some families could not afford medical care.

5. Why would mothers go to infant welfare clinics (Source 9)?

6. Name the new drugs which began to reduce common epidemic diseases at the end of the 1930s (Source 9).

7. What was a Poor Law funeral? Why was it 'a terrible disgrace' (Source 13)?

ASSESSMENT AND ANALYSIS

1. Contrast the advertisement for baby food (Source 2) with the evidence on child rearing in Source 1.

2. Why did the doctor in Source 3 believe that Marie Stopes was 'on the right lines'?

3. In what ways do Sources 7 and 9 agree on the conditions of work for doctors in the '20s and '30s?

4. How do Sources 10 to 15 suggest that funerals and attitudes towards death have changed in the last 50 years?

5. In Source 15 the priest suggests that there has been a decline in church-going. Can you think of ways of finding other evidence to support or oppose this claim?

EMPATHY

1. What would the mother in Source 1 have felt if she had read the Trufood advertisement (Source 2)?

2. In Source 3 why do you think the women students were 'dead against' Dr Stopes? Make a list of the arguments for and against birth control.

3. What improvements in social conditions and medical services would a family doctor have wished to see in this period? (See Sources 1, 3, 7 and 9.)

ORAL HISTORY ASSIGNMENT

Read about the introduction of the National Health Service in Britain after the Second World War.

What would you like to ask people who remember the coming of the NHS? Select the best questions devised by the whole class.

Using these questions interview one person each. In class compare the results of your interviews.

Your results could be presented as short essays on medicine in Britain before and after the coming of the National Health Service.

3 Childhood and School

Memories of childhood are often tinged with nostalgia for the lost innocence of youth. There are obvious dangers in using such evidence, yet certain themes emerge clearly.

Play was still seasonal. Toys were less sophisticated and often less expensive. Children in the 1920s and 1930s had books, magazines and comics, as well as more modern entertainment in cinema and radio. They were not yet exploited by slick advertising campaigns. Pop culture was still far in the future.

Buckets, spades and paddling. Some things don't change – but costumes do

CHILDHOOD

SOURCE 1

A housewife, daughter of a Yorkshire miner

My earliest memory as a child is of my father putting us out to be looked after. My mother had just died. . . I was brought up by my father, who was a collier. There were eight children; the eldest died as a baby. We were very poor, and had no toys. We ate bread and jam, mostly, but we always had one good dinner a day.

Window shopping – deprivation

SOURCE 2

A businessman who was brought up in the north of England. His father worked in a carpet mill

As a child I had a job – fetching washing, which my mother did for the better off. Father mended my boots with bits of leather from the mill. I had to polish my shoes every day, and my mother inspected them. I had patches in my trousers as big as a Union Jack, but I always went clean to school.

SOURCE 3

A shopkeeper's son, who became a hospital porter, remembers his childhood in a declining northern textile town

My parents kept an off-licence shop, and my friends' houses were completely different. One was a very big family. Every Friday night the children used to queue up for a bath in the kitchen sink. By the time they'd finished the water was so bloody thick you could roll it into balls. Their table was almost bare, but there was always a pot of treacle on it. They only had two bedrooms, so they used to sleep head to tail, five or six to a bed.

My parents weren't strict. I've had a good hiding many a time, but being sent to bed early hurt much more than a good hiding. We were never short of sweets, but if my father told us to do something we had to do it.

We were well off with rotten pears, broken biscuits and a pocketful of peas from the market.

We were always frightened of the local bobby, nicknamed 'Flash Harry'. If he saw you doing something, such as lighting cigs on the gas lamp, he gave you a real thrashing, but he never told your parents.

I only ever had one holiday with my parents, at Blackpool. We went and came back by taxi, but the driver was a friend, so it was free. I went on other holidays with my grandparents. I remember gambling on the amusement machines.

I used to read all the comics – *Beano, Dandy, Comic Cuts, Rover, Wizard* and *Hotspur*. Lord Snooty was my favourite character. And there was one character called 'Wilson'. He was always a great athlete, cricketer and footballer. He knocked down all the wickets in five minutes. If there were any free gifts going you had to fight to get into the shops.

Once we tried to form a scout group through the Vicar. I was in the church choir, so I had to go to church three times on Sunday, changing my clothes each time. This 'ere Vicar got us this room which we did up for the scouts. At weekends we used the room for playing cards, smoking and drinking beer from the off-licence. The Vicar came in and found us, and that was the end of the scouts for us.

I used to go on the annual Sunday School walks – at least twelve miles into the country from our town. We choir boys played an annual cricket match against the neighbouring parish church team. It usually ended up with fighting with bloody water pistols.

We used to go 'promming' – roaming round the town, looking for the nicest girls you could find. We went into pubs. You were always eighteen, whether you were or not.

SOURCE 4

A housewife remembers games in her Yorkshire childhood

We just played out – rounders, hop-scotch, skipping, netball. I won a medal for netball, but I've lost it. The police never bothered us. The farmers used to give us a piece of their field to play in. We played at tops and marbles, at bully and hoop, football and cricket.

SOURCE 5

A shopkeeper looks back on schoolboy amusements in a northern industrial town

We played street cricket, using dustbins as wickets. Our parents used to watch us. I was steeped in cricket. We went to the butcher's shop for a bladder, blew it up and used it for a football. On New Year's Day we went to the shops and called out. They threw out hot pennies. You used to pick them up and they burnt your bloody fingers.

You could run for bloody miles with a hoop and bully, made by the black-smith for 4d. We played with potties and glass allies. On Shrove Tuesday you had a whip and top, and you had to make a fancy coloured chalk design on the top.

potties and glass allies = marbles

A twelve-year-old girl changing bobbins in a cotton mill, 1920

SOURCE 6

A retired engineer, son of a Yorkshire shopkeeper, remembers his childhood

I was brought up with a strict moral code. Sunday School was compulsory. My parents were insistent on good behaviour and manners towards other people.

Once my mother sent me for some baby milk for my sister from the clinic. It was cheaper there, and I heard someone say so, so I wouldn't go there because I thought it was degrading to get something cheap.

The school dentist used to inspect us. He sent a card to my mother so that we could get free treatment, but I was not allowed to go to the school clinic. Other lads liked the time off school to go there, so I wanted to go, and I got my mother to agree. On the day I had to go by myself. It was a horrible place, a big Victorian house. As I went up to the door a boy came out, spitting blood. The nurse made me go in first. My gum was torn out – the dentist nearly pulled my head off. I didn't feel it degrading to go to the school dentist, but I did feel it so to get cheap milk.

Children were sent to houses to find out if neighbours needed anything doing. At night, in bed, I could hear the neighbours chatting. It was common to call at houses to see elderly people on the way home from school. One we called 'Grandma Sykes', although she was no relation. She used to play the piano and we sang hymns. We spent more time visiting relations – cousins were closer, there was more of a bond.

Middle-class children with an expensive toy car

Questions

UNDERSTANDING

1. What evidence of poverty is there in Sources 1, 2 and 3?

2. Make a list of the games mentioned in these extracts. What evidence is there that the games and amusements were less expensive then than now?

3. Why did the boy in Source 3 make neither a good scout nor a perfect choirboy?

4. Why was the boy in Source 6 frightened of the dentist? What does 'degrading' mean?

ASSESSMENT AND ANALYSIS

What evidence is there in these extracts to show that there was a strong sense of community and neighbourliness in the period? How reliable do you think this evidence is?

EMPATHY

What do these sources reveal about the nature of the parents' feelings towards their children?

School

Schooling for the bulk of the population was much more basic than today. Most children attended one school, the elementary school, from the age of five to fourteen. Here they were taught in very large classes (60 in a class was quite usual) and they learned only the most basic subjects.

Governments between the wars tried to increase the number of places in secondary schools. The Hadow Report of 1926 recommended a definite break between primary and secondary schools at the age of eleven. By the mid-1930s it was thought that there should be three types of secondary school – grammar, technical, and secondary modern. In many parts of the country these plans were not put into effect and children continued to go to the elementary schools.

In theory there was to be a ladder of opportunity which would enable poor but able children to work their way up to secondary schools and universities and colleges. In fact less than 1 in 100 ex-elementary school pupils entered English universities in 1934. It was much easier for the children of the wealthy at fee-paying schools outside the state system to reach the top rungs of the ladder.

Scotland had its own educational system. Secondary education had always been more common and many able children from working class homes did go to the Scottish universities.

A secondary school class in 1921

SOURCE 7
Extract from
the Hadow Report
of 1926

Until recent years, approximately ninety per
cent of children have received elementary
education up to the age of thirteen or fourteen,
and a small minority have been transferred to
secondary education . . . at about the age of
eleven.

SOURCE 8
A greengrocer's
son remembers

The Head wanted me to sit for a grammar school scholarship* but my
father was dead and I was the eldest. I wanted to take over the shop as soon
as possible.

*Places at some fee-paying schools were paid for by local education authorities

SOURCE 9
A builder's
merchant

One lad who was brilliant at school had a father who wouldn't work. The
Headmaster told the school that he'd have gone straight to the top, if he'd
had good parents.

SOURCE 10
A hospital porter
in the north
of England

At first I went to the church school. The teachers were good. You got
walloped for what you did, you knew you deserved it and you didn't
complain. One teacher knew we smoked – he used to call us out in class
and ask us for our cigs, to show us up. So we refused to play in his football
team until he gave us our cigs back.

Then I went to the secondary school. There was a vast difference. There
were science labs – we did experiments on rats and mice. Once, acting daft
in science, I turned my neighbour's gas tap on. He laid his head down, and
indirectly we bloody gassed him. It was ages before they got him right.

We had gardening sessions, and we had to bring our own implements.
Those who didn't have any had to be on their hands and knees, pulling the
bloody sods up. The vegetables went to the school kitchen.

We were taken on a trip to London. We saw the zoo and a printing works,
but to me London was just like any other town at that age. In fact, we felt
we'd been done – those who couldn't afford to go didn't have to write a
bloody essay on the trip.

SOURCE 11

Elementary
school children
in London,
about 1925

SOURCE 12

A retired
schoolmaster
from south
Yorkshire

I started my education at a private village school run by a spinster lady, but at about eight I went to the local elementary school. Most of the boys were miners' sons. We were well drilled in the 'three-Rs' and we had singing lessons. We learned quite a lot of surprisingly serious verse – I must have been only nine or ten when I learned passages from Shakespeare.

From this school I went to the local secondary school which later became a grammar school. It was an admirable school and by 1920 it had won several awards at Oxford and Cambridge, mainly for working-class pupils.

The masters were a tough lot – they had to be. Discipline could be severe. I saw one boy caned until his hand bled. Some of the boys were in rags, but I don't remember anyone complaining of being hungry, though I'm sure some were undernourished. This school pioneered the provision of school dinners, for which we paid five pence.

SOURCE 13

A solicitor's wife
who went to a
girls' boarding
school in
East Anglia

It was a church school. There was no corporal punishment, but things like disorder marks were terribly important, and to lose house marks was a degradation. The Headmistress was very strict. As the staff passed us in the corridor we pressed ourselves against the wall. We didn't mind this at all – manners matter. We had school meals with quite rigid rules on table manners – you couldn't use just a spoon for your pudding ('Surely you know better than that!'). You had to see that everyone had things before you, and be very polite at passing things. If you wanted a second helping, you asked the person next to you if *she* would like to have a second helping.

SOURCE 14

A civil engineer on his secondary school in the north-east

My secondary school was a Victorian building with no gym, no labs, no domestic science. On Friday afternoons we went to an old infirmary three miles away where there was a makeshift lab. The facilities were nil – we had to go to another school to do woodwork. An old chapel was eventually used as a gym, but the playing fields were 1½ miles away.

SOURCE 15

Portobello Road School, London, in the 1920s

SOURCE 16

An ironmonger who went to a northern grammar school

I was a bugger, but I was a good scholar. I was the one who saved folk if they were in trouble. One lad chloroformed himself, and I carried him downstairs and threw him in the toilet.

I saw masters knocked out. I was expelled from a class for a term. Others did worse than me – I only knocked him under the chin. The Great War brought foreigners as teachers. One was a nervous wreck – or he was when he left. We put a drawing pin on his chair *every* lesson. We put iron filings in sulphuric acid and it stank like the devil. He never found out. One day he just shut the bloody door and ran for his life.

Once a lad threw a lump of sodium into the swimming baths. He didn't know what it was and someone had dared him to do it. Smoke came up and the fire brigade were called out – they thought the bloody baths were on fire. Unfortunately he was expelled.

SOURCE 17

*A retired
headmaster from
Lancashire*

I went to school at five. It was a small chapel school on the fringes of the town. There were 90 children, with three teachers in three rooms. I was taught extremely well in an old-fashioned way. At nine years and ten months I won a scholarship to the grammar school. It was an unheard of thing.

I was expected to be top of the form, but emerged fourth and felt it a disgrace. Competition between boys was encouraged, but not in a very aggressive form. We had weekly cards and mark sheets. Every subject was given a grade, and if you got five excellent grades you were given a card. This fostered the idea of competition at a very early age.

SOURCE 18

*A sample of the
type of questions
used in intelligence
tests in Scotland
in the 1930s*

1. If 1/6th is larger than 1/5th write Q, if not write E.
2. If I am facing West with my arms stretched sideways, in what direction is my left arm pointing?
3. What is four times a quarter of four and a quarter?
4. Shakespeare was a great (SOLDIER, STATESMAN, POET) who lived in the reign of (HENRY VII, QUEEN ELIZABETH, QUEEN VICTORIA).

A classroom in 1936. These children appear smarter – evidence of the higher living standards in prosperous areas. Cheap school milk was available in the 1930s

Questions

UNDERSTANDING

1. Use Sources 7, 8 and 9 to explain why so many children did not go to secondary schools.

2. Why did the boy in Source 10 regret going on the trip to London?

3. In what ways did the witness in Source 12 (a) admire, and (b) disapprove of the schools he attended?

ASSESSMENT AND ANALYSIS

1. What evidence can you find in the extracts of strict discipline?

2. How do Sources 13 and 17 show that competition between pupils was encouraged?

3. List some ways in which schools in the 1920s and 1930s were less well-equipped than your own school.

4. Compare Sources 11 and 15. Do you think these children came from a rich or poor district? Give your reasons.

5. There are many written accounts of education in British 'public schools' in this period, but few of primary school education. Can you think of reasons for this?

EMPATHY

1. How would you describe the character of the boy in Source 10?

2. Answer the questions in Source 18. Discuss in class whether intelligence tests were a fair method of selecting children for different schools at the age of 11.

ORAL HISTORY ASSIGNMENTS

1. Talk to older members of your family about their childhood and education. What did they most enjoy and what did they most dislike about this period of their lives?

2. Invite former pupils of your school to visit your history class. Prepare in advance some questions you would like to ask them. Topics for discussion might include uniform, rules, subjects studied, games played and how the buildings have changed.

4 Family and Home

A Jubilee street party in Yorkshire, 1935

The normal social unit in Britain between the wars was the family, based on marriage. The size of the family was declining, for though many couples still had swarms of children, by 1938 the average number of children per marriage was just over two. The practice of birth control was spreading from the upper and middle to the working classes. Divorce was still rare, but it was on the increase. In 1938 there were 7000 divorces – nine times as many as in 1914.

The ideal of the family and marriage was treated with an almost sacred respect and reverence by politicians, preachers and the press. Our interviews revealed another ideal – that of 'good neighbourliness' and a sense of 'community'. Families helped each other, sharing problems and pleasures. British society between the wars was not made up of individuals thrown together like grains of sand.

One of the main achievements in social reform was to improve the housing stock. Financial aid from central government enabled local authorities to build council estates which were a vast improvement upon the urban slums created by industrialisation. The growth of private enterprise house building created solid, suburban semi-detached and detached houses at reasonable prices.

COURTSHIP

SOURCE 1
A London housewife

We were courting for two years. We had our arguments – I should say we did. We nearly broke it off once over whether we should go to the opera or the pictures.

He had Wednesday afternoons off and he used to come and meet me. Sam wanted to see *Così Fan Tutte* at Sadler's Wells, but I wanted to see a picture at the King's Cross cinema – *Call It A Day* with Ian Hunter. I didn't think he'd leave me to go by myself, and we had a row about it in the Corner House restaurant, Islington. I was determined not to give way to him.

I wrote him a letter the next evening – he's still got it after nearly 50 years. I told him it was better to part – it had nothing to do with his family, we just had different ideas on things, I said. But of course we got together again. That's the only time I ever wrote him a letter, I think.

SOURCE 2
A civil servant in London

He was jumping on a tram at dinner-time. I discovered he worked in my department at the Post Office. We met on the stairs and said hello, and he asked me to look up a non-existent query, and then he asked me out. The first time I couldn't go. Eventually I did.

When I went to meet him there he was with a Triumph two-seater, and I had to explain that father wouldn't let me out for long. It was eight-thirty, and father said I had to be home by nine. We broke through at Christmas when father asked him in for a drink. Our courtship lasted eight years. Then the war jerked us into marriage – you thought anything might happen, and by this time he was 37.

SOURCE 3
A domestic servant meets a Yorkshire miner

I met my husband in the pub, although I didn't drink. We were courting three years. I got on with him when I was seventeen. I got on well with his mother. She fed me and we helped her. We used to go for long walks – we could never afford to ride on the buses. We went to the pictures but he used to fall asleep.

A London courting couple in the 1930s. He was a hairdresser, she a typist. (See Sources 5 and 10)

SOURCE 4
A London civil servant (see also Source 2)

We always had enough money to enjoy ourselves. When we went to a dance, we always went in evening dress. Ladies' Night at the Freemasons' Lodge came once a year. A red-coated Master of Ceremonies announced your names. You had cocktails. A board showed the seating plan. There was an enormous thirteen course dinner, with a sorbet in the middle. There was one waiter to every four people, two bands for dancing, reception rooms with settees and coal fires. I danced with 'Uncle Mac' of *Children's Hour*. You held your partner and loved her in those days. Carriages came at two o' clock, and there was soup before you left. Every woman got a beautiful gift.

SETTING UP HOUSE

SOURCE 5

A typist and a barber in London

We saved up for furniture – I used to buy my stuff at Woolworth's. I was only on a small wage. Father-in-law bought us the kitchen furniture – plain wood. My mother and dad bought us candlesticks, the Jewish custom in those days. I had a lovely ring. He saved up for ages – a solitaire, one and a half carat, worth 50 pounds – but he got it in the trade for a bit less. He was determined to give me a lovely ring.

SOURCE 6

A Yorkshire cloth dyer

We were courting for six years, saving to get married. Well, you see, we needed a deposit for the house and payments for the furniture. We sometimes went to the pictures. It was a shilling in the circle and eightpence in the stalls. We saved fourpence by going in the stalls when we got serious about getting married.

Clothes were a big item. I spent a lot of money on them before my courting days. Then I went to Burton's when I started feeling the pinch. But money went further in those days. We had a new house – we watched it being built. It was £530 for a three-bedroomed detached house.

SOURCE 7

An accountant in Yorkshire

We bought a new house a few months before our marriage. It was £449 for a three-bedroomed semi. I got a pound knocked off because there wasn't a light over the pantry.

SOURCE 8

A Yorkshire miner

We easily found a house to rent. We paid for the furniture over four months. A double bed was nine pounds, but extra for the mattress. We got lino – inlaid – 25 square yards, including fitting, all for five pounds – a lot of money in those days.

SOURCE 9

A northern businessman

We rented a back-to-back house for 3s. 9d. a week. It had an outside dry toilet. There was a 'best' room with a fireplace and red plush curtains and a big aspidistra. The other room was for everyday, everything – living, eating, cooking.

The neighbours were smashing. They all helped each other. It was a good spirit. They were the happiest days of your life, when you had nothing and you had to struggle for everything.

THE WEDDING

It wasn't a big wedding, just a few friends and family – about 50. We had a tea dance with supper in the evening.

My wedding dress was white and silver lamé – a silver fern design, with a neckline like a lily, folded over in petals. It had long sleeves and a tulip line. My sisters were bridesmaids, and they wore white taffeta dresses, with violet jackets and head-dresses. My little brother was a page boy – he wore an Eton suit with long trousers.

I had a pure silk going-away outfit – a black and white two-piece suit, with a big picture hat. We saved up to go to Bournemouth for our honeymoon. The hotel's not there now, but it was marvellous – the food was so good.

A small working-class wedding

SOURCE 11

The miner's wife (see Sources 3 and 8)

We got married in Chapel and had the reception at home. It was just a little cake. His mother paid for everything. Just as we got married the owner of the pit where my husband worked committed suicide – he hung himself. I had to go and ask for my job back.

An upper-class wedding group

The wedding photograph of two Yorkshire woollen mill workers

Questions

UNDERSTANDING

1. How long were the engagements described in Sources 1, 2 and 3?

2. What problems faced the courting couples in Sources 1, 2 and 3?

3. How did the outbreak of war affect the courtship in Source 2?

4. Describe three ways in which the couples in Sources 5, 6 and 7 economised.

5. Make a sketch of your impression of the bride's dress described in Source 10.

ASSESSMENT AND ANALYSIS

1. After reading these extracts explain why you think engagements between the wars were often lengthy.

2. What evidence is there in Sources 3 and 4 to show that the couples involved came from very different backgrounds?

3. What different kinds of housing are referred to in Sources 6, 7, 8 and 9?

EMPATHY

1. What do the sources show us about the attitudes of courting couples towards each other and about their future expectations?

2. The number of divorces was much smaller then than now. Can you think of any reasons for this?

Proud parents with daughter, 1930s

THE ABDICATION

One particular marriage which has left vivid memories was that between Edward VIII (later the Duke of Windsor) and Mrs Wallis Simpson.

Edward's father, George V, had been a very popular king, a devoted family man, and the Royal Family was regarded as an ideal, model family.

Edward had been king for less than a year when a sensational crisis arose over his choice of wife. The Prime Minister, Stanley Baldwin, firmly believed that Edward could not remain king if he married a twice-divorced American. Baldwin claimed to have the backing of the governments of the Empire, the support of the churches, and the working classes in the north of England.

Edward decided to sacrifice his throne. He abdicated in favour of his brother on 11 December 1936, declaring that: 'I have found it impossible . . . to discharge my duties as king as I would wish to do without the help and support of the woman I love.' He went into exile and married Mrs Simpson a year later.

The crisis pointed to a stark contrast between public duty and private life. Even 50 years later the rights and wrongs are discussed with lively emotion.

Edward VIII making his first radio broadcast as King

SOURCE 12
Sandy Powell,
a variety and
radio comedian

I used to do an hour's show on the radio in the 1930s – *Pages from Sandy's Album* – I suppose it was on nearly every week. In those days there were no recordings – it was all live. Well, we were doing an hour's show, to be on the air 8.30 to 9.30.

When we arrived to do the show the producer said, 'Sandy, I've got some rather unpleasant news. We're not putting your show out tonight.' I said, 'Why? It's not as bad as that, is it?' He said, 'No, but we've had to put someone else on instead.' I thought they'd got a new comedian, so I said, 'Who is it?' He said, 'The King.'

That night we went to see the Crazy Gang at the Palladium. They broadcast the abdication speech live to the audience in the theatre. You can imagine the emotion. After the show I took my kids to a restaurant to have a meal. The waiter said, 'I thought you were supposed to be on the wireless tonight.' I said, 'Yes, but the King was on instead.' This Italian waiter said, 'Funny people the English. In my country, if the King came on the wireless, we would all be shooting each other.'

SOURCE 13
A Newcastle
shop assistant

People cried at Edward VIII's abdication broadcast. He was much preferred to George VI. George was admired for trying to overcome his speech impediment. But Edward was royalty with a problem normal to ordinary people. There was sympathy for a loser.

SOURCE 14
The wife of a
Yorkshire solicitor

I remember vividly listening to Edward's farewell abdication speech. I regarded him as a pin-up, a film star. I was eating an egg, listening to his farewell speech and weeping. I felt he was wrong. He shattered all our feelings about him. He ought to have given her up and stayed on as King. I thought he would have done.

SOURCE 15
A mill worker
in Yorkshire

Edward himself was very popular. We bought an ashtray with his picture on it, down at the Co-op. My friend said, 'Oh, we're not going to put our ash on him.'

SOURCE 16
A Durham
coal miner

I felt very sympathetic to Edward. He loved that woman and did what he thought was right. I'd met him in France in the First World War – he stopped to talk to us when we were on guard.

SOURCE 17
A Yorkshire shopkeeper

Edward VIII was generally liked. It was the high-ups that shoved him out. They had divorces among themselves. In the workers' eyes, he had a right to marry who he wanted. He was well-liked. He used to look at broken-down houses in Wales. He'd have made a good King.

SOURCE 18
A Lancashire headmaster

My parents didn't approve of Mrs Simpson. Their attitude, purely practical, was that Edward was being a bloody fool.

SOURCE 19
A Yorkshire mill owner

The women were broken-hearted. As far as we were concerned, it made no difference. Only the older ones thought it disgraceful to marry a divorcee.

SOURCE 20
A Yorkshire miner

Edward VIII was a very good man. I don't see why he shouldn't have been allowed to marry and carry on as King. He stood by his own principles and married the woman he loved. I wouldn't want to do away with the monarchy. They can't help being what they are.

SOURCE 21
A Labour councillor in the north of England

Edward VIII came on a visit when he was Prince of Wales. I thought he was drunk and it was only 10.30 in the morning. When I hear the word Royalty I immediately think 'parasites'. They're only ordinary folk, and all this adulation is meaningless.

Edward VIII and Mrs Simpson on holiday in August 1936

Questions

UNDERSTANDING

1. Why was Sandy Powell told that his radio show was cancelled (Source 12)?

2. What does 'adulation' mean (Source 21)?

3. What evidence is there in these sources to show that the issue was a very emotional one?

ASSESSMENT AND ANALYSIS

1. Why did Edward VIII decide to abdicate?

2. Which of these extracts is neutral and gives no opinion about the rights and wrongs of the issue?

3. What impression of Edward have you formed from reading these extracts?

4. Why would a historian need to exercise great care in using oral evidence on the abdication?

ORAL HISTORY ASSIGNMENT

Collect memories of the abdication crisis of 1936. What are people's attitudes towards Edward, Mrs Simpson and other members of the Royal Family?

DOMESTIC ROUTINE

SOURCE 22

A Yorkshire housewife recalling housework in her childhood

'Fettling' is the old Yorkshire word for housework. I remember my auntie before the First World War – she cleaned up as most people did in those days. On Saturday lunchtime they brought out the brass fire-irons and the best fringed rug, the best cushions, the best plush table cover with a red fringe. On Monday morning the brass fire-irons were cleaned, wrapped in brown paper and put out of sight, the rug rolled up and put away, and a wooden fender and a rag rug brought out for the week. If they had a stair carpet they used to put white cloth on the stairs, taken up every two weeks to wash. This was fettling when I was a girl.

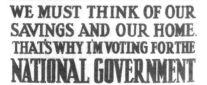

The Conservative-dominated National Government of the 1930s appealed to housewives and mothers in their election posters

SOURCE 23

The same housewife recalls her own experiences

When I became a housewife I had no brass fire-irons. Housework had become a bit easier. There was less scrubbing and polishing. We still had brass handles on the oven door to clean, but we didn't cover the stair carpet. A carpet sweeper was for the well-off – most of us used a hard carpet brush.

We scrubbed steps and window sills and put white scouring on. Some people painted their steps white. Coal cellar grates were black-leaded, with lino and a brick on top. Decorating was more thorough. People mostly did their own. The ceiling was whitewashed once a year – gas dirtied the ceilings.

Electricity was immediately popular – it was more convenient, but it was of little importance for anything except lighting at first. There were no electrical appliances. I got my first electric washing machine about 1936. It was made locally and it cost £33 but it lasted 30 years. Many people at the time were buying American machines, which couldn't be repaired.

SOURCE 24
A publican's wife in Cheshire

I knew I was going to stay at home. Mother was waiting for me to get finished at school so that I could stay at home and help her, because she had my brothers and sisters and father to look after. They were all working, and I helped in the house until I was eighteen.

I helped her with the baking, washing and cleaning. When I got done I went out. My pocket money was four shillings a week, but she bought all my clothes, you know.

SOURCE 25
Advertisement from Punch, *10 June 1936*

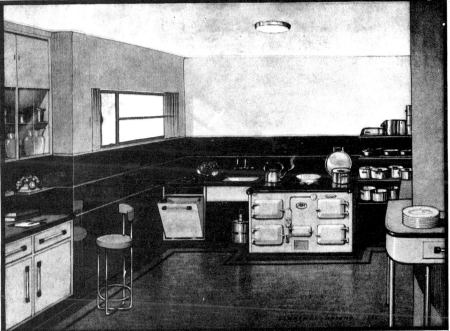

Kitchen design by Mrs. Darcy Braddell.   *Drawing by Lawrence Wright.*

The Aga Cooker - the heart of a planned kitchen

SOURCE 26
A Yorkshire greengrocer

Housewives had a routine; washday Monday, baking Thursday, black-leading Friday. Washing took all day – sink, fire, mangle, posser, rubbing board. You froze all day with clothes round the fire. There was always meat and potato pie on Thursday. Everybody did these things – it was a ritual.

posser = a pounding instrument used in washing

Making do. A Stepney mother

SOURCE 27

*An east Yorkshire
farmer's daughter*

We kept hens and ducks. Food was good – plain and wholesome, and plenty of it. We had a huge joint of beef on a Sunday. The workers were fed just as well as us.

I was always determined not to be tied to a routine like my mother, but Monday was still washday.

We both did the shopping. I expected to be properly treated in shops, not like the matey fashion of today.

There were no convenience foods. We were expected to make our own – bread, jam, everything. We would never have dreamed of buying anything which we could make ourselves.

In shops 30 or 40 years ago one met a real politeness, a real willingness to be of service. Now it is rather rude and off-hand, a cold, negligent attitude.

SOURCE 28

*A Durham
miner's wife*

I had a coal fire with a range. I had to clean it twice a week. The fire was never out. We got electricity just after we were married but I had no proper washing machine until later.

For food we had pig cheeks, fat and bread, pork scratchings, black pudding, tripe. My husband was only a miner. I baked my own bread, and he grew vegetables and flowers. We hardly bought any fruit, no tins. We had rice puddings a lot.

Questions

UNDERSTANDING

1. In what ways had housework become easier for the housewife in Source 23 than for her auntie in Source 22?

2. Why was this housewife (Source 23) so pleased with her washing machine?

3. Why did the young man in Source 2 dislike Mondays?

ASSESSMENT AND ANALYSIS

1. What cleaning jobs described in Source 23 would probably be regarded as unnecessary today?

2. Look at the kitchen in Source 25. The Aga cooker was very expensive, but what conveniences does the kitchen lack which we might expect today?

EMPATHY

Write an advertisement by a firm selling electrical washing machines in the 1930s.

5 Earning a Living

A short 're-stocking' boom in Britain's major industries followed the First World War. Yet these 'staple' industries – coal, iron, steel, engineering, ship-building and textiles – on which the first Industrial Revolution had been based quickly suffered depression and unemployment. They became 'ailing giants'.

The demands of war had given a temporary and artificial stimulus to many industries, disguising weaknesses in organisation, technology and manpower which had already begun to worry some observers before 1914. When international trade was forced into new patterns by war these weaknesses became clear. Out-of-date machinery, small units of production, a militant but underskilled labour force, insufficient capital investment – all these common handicaps led to a drastic decline in the exports so vital to their prosperity. World demand was no longer growing for the goods which Britain specialised in producing. The war had stimulated foreign competition in some industries. Britain suffered a declining share of a declining market.

Each of the staple industries had its own specific, particular problems and the fall in both international and domestic demand led to severe unemployment in the areas in which they were located – parts of the 'Celtic fringe' of Scotland, South Wales and Northern Ireland; the north-east; parts of Lancashire and Yorkshire; parts of the Midlands.

Yet Britain was by no means a waste land of slump and jobless. Some areas prospered because they were able to attract a different type of industry. Improvements in road transport and electrical power freed these 'new' industries from the old deciding factors of location – the railways and the coal fields. The south-east, the areas around London and other great conurbations, parts of the Midlands – these regions enjoyed high wages and almost full employment in the expanding electrical industry, motor car and aeroplane manufacture, chemicals and plastics. Consumer goods and services, such as food, drink, tobacco, printing, dyes, bricks, pottery, glass and building also enjoyed growth and prosperity. The two nations of rich south and poor north became more evident in the 1920s and 1930s.

SOURCE 1

Extract from The Social Structure of England and Wales, *by A.M. Carr-Saunders and D. Caradog Jones, 1937*

In 1931, out of every 100 occupied persons in the whole country, 51, approximately one-half were engaged in making and producing things:

producing hay, corn, potatoes, sheep and oxen on the land; fishing for salmon, plaice and herring in the sea; burrowing in the interior of the earth for coal and iron; fashioning wood and metal in workshops into machinery, furniture and ornaments; weaving wool and cotton into fabrics in mills; building houses, manufacturing clothes, boots and crockery, implements, toys, every imaginable and unimaginable thing.

Twenty-three out of every 100, nearly one quarter of the total, were engaged in buying and selling . . . and in moving by road, rail or water, all those things to warehouses, shops and houses as required: this group also includes people concerned with finance and insurance.

Thirteen out of every 100 waited upon, or prepared food, drink, and sometimes lodging for the other workers and for the idlers, to provide for their bodily needs and comforts.

Six out of every 100 were engaged in administrative jobs, such as the civil service and Post Office.

Three out of every 100 were ministers, doctors, teachers and lawyers.

One out of every 100 was enrolled for the defence of the State.

SOURCE 2

The Pupil's
Empire Atlas,
1925

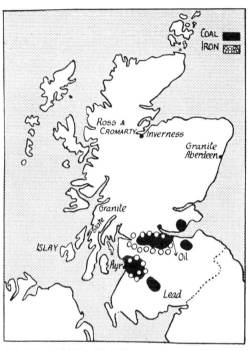

COAL AND IRON

MANUFACTURES

MINING

In the late eighteenth and nineteenth centuries the Industrial Revolution in Britain was fuelled by coal. By 1913 production of coal reached a record level of 287 million tons and the industry employed more men than any other. It then went into decline. Between the wars production fell sharply (to 164 million tons by 1921) and the wages and jobs of miners were under constant threat. Many towns and villages on the coalfields were entirely dependent on the mines. Sons naturally followed their fathers into the only local industry. As demand for coal fell, whole communities suffered.

British coal-mines were privately owned. During the years of decline the owners could not afford the mechanisation and improvements which the workers thought necessary. Relations between miners and owners were often bitter (see pp. 63–69 on 'The General Strike'). The miners' unions demanded nationalisation, but this was postponed until after the Second World War.

SOURCE 3

A Durham miner describes how he entered the industry

I left school at fourteen – we were all pleased to leave school and get a job. My father was a miner and we lived in a house owned by the colliery.

The first day I went by myself into the pit. It was an eight-hour shift. I was the driver, a pony driver. We got very little training, you were taught by whoever took you on.

My wage at fourteen was a pound a week. It was pretty good at that time – a mill wage was only fourteen shillings.

A pony-driver, about 1920

SOURCE 4

Going down the pit – a Yorkshire miner

You went down the pit in cages. Once we were shooting up, and it went extra fast when it should have been slowing down. It suddenly stopped dead just below the top and threw us all about. We might have overshot the wheels. We stayed there half an hour – swinging between heaven and hell – while they got the thing right.

When you got down, the distance from the shaft to the face could easily be a mile and half. And you didn't get paid for that walking time, travelling to and fro. You took your food, your 'snap', down with you. I used to have a sandwich in my snap tin and a bottle of tea. Chewing tobacco was common – they said it helped them get rid of the dust out of their mouths.

A miner eats his tea

SOURCE 5

At work in a Yorkshire mine

All they wanted was a good hard worker. It was still all picks and hand getting. There were no machines.

We were fighting for a living. Miners had to pull bloody great six hundred-weight tubs with sharp iron corners. It was mainly piece-work – the more coal you got, the more money you got, and the owners liked it. Men of 50 or 60, not as fast as someone of 25, were expected to do as much as anyone. But there was a minimum wage-rate you couldn't fall under, because some places were very hard going. Some miners got soft, easy coal and a high wage; some had to get hard coal. The mine was never still, even at weekends. We worked Saturdays and sometimes Sunday mornings.

SOURCE 6

A Yorkshire miner describes the hazards of his work

There were accidents all the time, usually nothing much – broken legs or trapped fingers. If you had your fingers on the tub and the roof was low it would trap your hand if you weren't sharp enough to get it off.

The first day at one pit I went down and saw some of the men smoking! They used candles to light that pit, and we had to pay for them to make sure we didn't use too many. This was about 1930. Well, I expected the deputy to fine the men for smoking, and he came along smoking his pipe. I didn't stay there long.

My father was the engine winding man – he wound the cage up and down. He liked to have a drink of beer in the engine house. One day Tommy Haig came in and drank what he thought was my father's beer. It was vitriol. It burnt his insides out and he died almost instantly. If my father drank too much my mother had to wind the cage up.

There were lots of accidents. One man was squashed between two tubs. The signal to have the tub sent down was a tap on the rails. This chap knocked the rail by accident and the tub was sent down and killed him. He was chewing tobacco – most of us did – and the force of the tub squashing him sent the tobacco flying out of his mouth and it landed bang in the middle of his cap.

Helmets weren't compulsory so I didn't wear one. We had some soft caps instead. Once I was making a water gully and I misjudged the speed of the drill. It kicked back and the handle split my head open. When I took the cap off blood was pouring out. I refused to go to the doctor's because I was going to Wembley to see the Rugby League Cup Final the following day, and I didn't want him to tell me to stop at home. The deputy said, 'Tha must 'ave a bloody 'ead like iron, Jimmy; tha's broken t' 'andle off t' borer.'

The boilers at the pit had steam gauges, but no valves. There were wooden pegs pulled out by tongs and replaced with a hammer to regulate the pressure. Why there wasn't an explosion I'll never know. Well, there was an explosion eventually, that's what closed it down, but I wasn't there then.

SOURCE 7
Working conditions in the Yorkshire coalfield in the 1920s

There was never any chance to get out of the pits. You could move from one pit to another, without much improvement.

Your back used to be grazed, with lumps like buttons from the top to the bottom. There were no pit baths at first. We used to have a big tin bath at home in front of the fire. When the baths came they were a great benefit – you didn't like travelling home on the buses before, dirtying them. You don't know whether they've been to work or to church today, miners.

There was no resentment against the employers. We were all in favour of nationalisation; it was seen as a chance of betterment.

There were no cap lamps. We had heavy safety lamps. We put a handkerchief or strap round our neck and hung the lamp on, but we had to be very steady or it went out. If it went out you might have to go two or three hundred yards to find a lighter.

I've worked in water many a time. It used to come down like rain through the roof. We used to have to take changes of clothing in a leather sack. The wife used to wash and dry clothes in rotation. You got none provided by the mines until nationalisation. I've seen myself knee-deep in water. It's not very nice – you couldn't change your trousers before the shift finished.

Before the days of pit-head baths

Questions

UNDERSTANDING

1. What are the different types of manufacturing production described in Source 1?

2. What percentage of the population of England and Wales were in the armed forces?

3. Why had textile industries developed on the coalfields of northern England and Scotland? (Source 2.) What was the main industry in your part of the country in 1926? What is the main industry now?

4. In Source 3 why did the miner prefer his job to one in a mill?

5. Why did miners commonly chew tobacco?

6. 'It was mainly piece-work.' (Source 5). What is piece-work?

7. Why did the miner in Source 6 refuse to go to the doctor's?

ASSESSMENT AND ANALYSIS

1. What evidence is there in Sources 3 to 7 that miners considered their work difficult?

2. Using Sources 6 and 7, show ways in which the mining industry could be considered primitive and backward in this period.

3. Give three reasons why coal mines were so dangerous in the 1920s and 1930s. Can you think of any other common dangers, not mentioned in these sources?

EMPATHY

1. Explain why a miner might try to discourage his son from entering the mine.

2. Explain why a young school leaver might still wish to follow his father into mining.

3. Write a letter from a doctor in a mining village in which you discuss the effect of working in the mine upon the health of your patients.

TEXTILES

The two most important textile industries were cotton in Lancashire and woollens in Yorkshire. The cotton industry had always depended on exports, but the war affected its international markets. In the 1920s exports fell sharply: Japan and India developed their own industries, using new machinery and cheaper labour. Many of the cotton towns of Lancashire suffered massive unemployment.

Military demand for uniforms and blankets had created great profits in the woollen industry of the West Riding of Yorkshire, but after 1918 the normal peacetime market was much smaller. Declining foreign demand and obsolete machinery led to unemployment. Another factor was the growth in popularity of artificial fibres such as rayon and nylon, a result of progress in the chemical industry.

Lancashire weavers in the 1930s. The machinery is hardly modern

SOURCE 8

A Yorkshire mill girl

I was a weaver in the mill. Aye, I was in the union. There was this strike once, but the union money ran out after a week, so we never joined any more after that. It was a big mill with over four hundred workers. The manager was strict – if you weren't in at 6 o' clock in the morning they locked the gates and you had to wait until 8.30 to get in. We got up at 5 o' clock to walk three miles, in thick snow in winter, to get there. We wore big boots and hand-knitted black wool stockings. For six shillings a week.

SOURCE 9

A mill owner's son in the West Riding of Yorkshire, who later took over the firm

I went to work in my father's firm which produced fairly cheap cloth and we did our own dyeing. All our machinery was English but the dyes were German. We had our own dye-house, with vats and poles. The tubs were big enough to swim in – I used to swim in them at weekends. The machinery was always breaking down, and it had to be repaired by a full-time engineer.

I had to go to night classes at technical college to learn chemistry and dyeing, three nights a week.

We employed about 25 people. Ninety per cent of our workers stayed with us all their working lives. We were non-union. We opposed unions then and I still do now. Workers just asked for so much more wage – they

A woollen spinner in Yorkshire

haggled and we negotiated, but they never stopped work. Some women worked for us for 35 years. They might come to us for tea, and we sent them a bird at Christmas.

There was no hostility to me as the employer's son. I was a worker with a pair of clogs on. I started at seven like them. Our house was near the works – work was always with us. I got fifteen shillings a week, but some workers got two pounds a week. I was poorly paid in comparison to the workers – that was my father's idea.

We never had any serious accidents. We had to get water from a well: the engineer went down in a bucket, which was a bit dangerous (someone once threw a stink bomb after him). We used to recycle rags into a cloth called 'shoddy', and people got skin ailments from the dust in the rags. We used hydrochloric acid to destroy any cotton in the rags: it destroyed men too after twenty years – at least, their teeth dropped out.

SOURCE 10
The chief dyer in a Yorkshire mill

In the bottom dye-house the pans were too low. One of my dyers was wearing clogs; he slipped and fell into the pan and was boiled to death. Stricter safety regulations were just creeping in before the Second World War.

Mill-workers celebrating the 21st birthday of their boss's daughter

SOURCE 11
*A Lancashire
Labour councillor,
now retired*

Working people were aware of great difference between those at the top and themselves. But work in the mill was not hard – there was no driving, no conveyor belt. Quite truthfully there was a happy, contented atmosphere. There was also hardship, but there was no feeling of rebellion or revolt, which irritated me as a socialist.

Questions

UNDERSTANDING

1. Describe some of the dangers of work in textile manufacturing (Sources 9 and 10).

2. How was lateness punished (Source 8)?

ASSESSMENT AND ANALYSIS

1. What different attitudes to trade unions are shown by Sources 8 and 9?

2. What differences in the way workers are treated in large and in small firms could be deduced from Sources 8 and 9?

Ring-spinning was faster and cheaper than mule-spinning – but Lancashire firms were slow to introduce new machinery

FARMING

During the First World War British farmers had been encouraged to grow more food so that the country would not be totally dependent on imports when ships were in danger from German submarine attacks. Prices and profits had been guaranteed by the government, minimum wages for farm workers established and improved methods of marketing introduced.

After the war this protection and encouragement finished when industrial depression set in. The farming industry felt betrayed as it was again left to face the full and icy blasts of competition from cheap imported food which could be easily obtained.

Farming was still labour intensive in spite of increasing mechanisation. Almost one million men worked in agriculture, nearly as many as in mining.

SOURCE 12

Extract from The Social Structure of England and Wales, *by Carr-Saunders and Caradog Jones*

Twenty-four per cent of the men engaged in agriculture are fifty-five years of age or over; at first sight this is surprising, because agricultural work involves hard physical labour. But it is a healthy occupation; moreover it cannot be much speeded up and is not performed in gangs. Therefore an elderly man does not find himself unable to stand the pace.

SOURCE 13

This retired teacher used to visit his uncle's farm in the north-east of Scotland in the 1930s, when he was a young schoolboy

The farmhouse and outbuildings were something out of Dickens. There was a workshop knee-deep in sawdust. The farm hands lived in bothies – two rooms with a central door; one contained a mother, father and seven children. It was really remarkable how orderly the rooms were, with no gas, no electricity and only pumped water.

There was an almost medieval system of barter. Uncle had very little money and exchanged potatoes for things. Aunt's housekeeping was what she made on eggs. She made her own butter. The diet was very restricted – soup, rabbit (for lunch, every day) with curds. The whole community used to meet at regular intervals at fêtes. The village is now derelict.

An agricultural demonstration in Berkshire in 1930. A horse ploughman inspects a tractor plough

SOURCE 14

A housewife who was brought up on a farm in the East Riding of Yorkshire

There was still a squire in our village. He read the lesson in church each week. There was his big house in the middle of the village, overlooking everything.

SOURCE 15

Extract from a speech, 'On England', made by the Prime Minister, Stanley Baldwin, in 1924

To me, England is the country, and the country is England . . . The sounds of England, the tinkle of the hammer on the anvil in the country smithy, the corncrake on a dewy morning, the sound of the scythe against the whetstone, and the sight of a plough team coming over the brow of a hill, the sight that has been seen in England since England was a land, and may be seen in England long after the Empire has perished. . . . The wild anemones in the woods in April, the last load at night of hay being drawn down a lane as the twilight comes on. . . . These things strike down to the very depths of our nature.

Questions

UNDERSTANDING

1. Why were more than one in five farm labourers over 55 years of age (Source 12)?

2. Explain 'medieval system of barter' and 'derclict' (Source 13).

ASSESSMENT AND ANALYSIS

What evidence is there in Sources 12 to 15 that farming was still old-fashioned and traditional in some areas between the wars?

SERVICES

For those in employment wages were good. They could afford some pleasures which would earlier have been considered luxuries.

There was an increasing number of workers who offered services rather than produced goods.

The labour force grew in transport, hotels, restaurants, cinemas, theatres, shops and garages. Newspapers increased in circulation and magazines and books sold more easily – a new product of this period was the paperback book.

SOURCE 16

A Yorkshire ironmonger

I was doing the bloody lot. My job was 24 hours a day. Plumbers used to come in the middle of the night, throwing stones at my bedroom window. I had to get up in snow. I had to go and get them tubing and piping to get emergency jobs done. They wouldn't wait till morning. The plumber had always to be 'on tap'!

SOURCE 17

A poulterer's wife in Yorkshire

People didn't realise the work that went into preparing for Christmas. We bought the turkeys live and kept them in a pen at the back of the Prospect Inn. The week before Christmas my husband was up killing, plucking and dressing the birds till 3 o'clock in the morning. His brother went to bed on Christmas Eve with swollen legs, completely exhausted, and didn't get up again until the holiday was over and it was time to open the shop again. And they all thought we were making a fortune; but for two weeks after Christmas nobody bought anything.

SOURCE 18

The manager of a Co-operative store in west Yorkshire, now retired

There just isn't as much work today. You used to have to make bags yourself. Everything was to weigh. If someone wanted an ounce of pepper you'd to make a bag and weigh it up. One old lass, she always got a ten stone bag of flour, once a fortnight – I had to stagger up with this ten stone bag of flour.

Everything was fresh. They got cheaper cuts of meat, but they knew what to do with them. You knew everybody and you talked to them.

It was all 'tick'. Everybody had a week's credit. There wasn't one in a hundred that was a cash customer. They came on Friday and paid the bill, then took a load of tick. There was a lot of midnight flitting.

With shopkeepers it was the simplest thing in the world to alter a pair of scales or put your thumb on the scales. Yeast came in a seven pound sack. It started drying out. So they wrapped it up and dropped it in a bowl of water – to make it weigh more, you know.

Woolworth's assistants

SOURCE 19

A Yorkshire greengrocer

I left school at fourteen to go carting for my father. It was a sort of mobile shop – fish, fruit and vegetables. I was always running after the bloody horse!

On the horse and cart you had to start getting ready at 7 o'clock and leave at 9. You finished at 5, tea-time. The first job on a morning was to catch the bloody horse. That was a hell of a job. In winter the horse always had a bran mash. It went to the blacksmith's once every three months for new shoes. We bought the bran and chop for the horse from the local coal merchant. Shovelling shit on a morning – that was another job!

Every Monday we had to change all the papers in the boxes on the cart. It was only newspaper but it took all morning. Monday afternoon was half-day. Hygiene? Out with a horse and cart, pouring with rain, everything wet through! We carried four hundredweight of spuds on the back. We came in at night soaked to the skin. In winter we had lamps with candles in; the wind blew the bloody candles out. Once the horse bolted and smashed the bloody lot up outside the pub; that didn't happen very often, but when it did it caused some damage.

You could get a decent rabbit for 9d. We dressed them on the cart; they were hung round the cart in their skins. Local moggies used to come round the cart waiting for the scraps; if you weren't careful they'd jump on the cart for fish. It wasn't an easy life.

I wore a khaki smock and a blue apron with pockets in the front. I was never allowed to keep the notes – my uncle took charge of them.

There was lots of competition, especially in hawking. But there was no real hostility. We would find out each other's prices. There was no code of conduct at all – the streets were full of horses and carts, hawking stuff.

My father tendered for a shop on High Street. He made the biggest offer – a pound a week. It had two windows, in the middle of the town. It was a gold mine. When a shopkeeper was successful he took another shop, then another, until someone diddled him.

I went into the shop at eighteen. The horse and cart finished when the war started. In those days a horse and cart took a lot more than a shop. In the shop you spent hours doing nowt. In winter we spent hours throwing a lemon to one another to keep warm. We didn't close till nine – and of course people came at the last minute.

The wholesale market started at 5.30. My father got the early tram down. Then they delivered the stuff in motor wagons. They were all sharks at the market. These local markets have declined; they were thriving then. There were twelve wholesalers here then; now there's only one. This is due to the car – everyone can go farther afield.

Some areas were very poor. People lived in cellar kitchens. They never saw daylight, like bloody rabbits living in a warren. They lived four or five steps below ground. They all stuck together though, great sense of community.

We had the snob types coming in. One woman had a little Highland terrier which went for your heels. One day I hit it with a bucket – she'd have sacked us straight away if she'd seen me. Some of the snobs we called 'sir' or 'madam'. You rarely saw a man in a shop in those days. These people had cheap domestics from Barnsley or Doncaster [mining areas], even in ordinary houses – they were fed and clothed for a pittance, working morning till night. At least I was independent – not ruled by a mill bugger.

There was lots of class distinction. At the Grange people were doing us a favour to buy from us; the lower grade customer was glad to see us come round.

Friday was the main shopping day, when they got paid. A weekend order – well, ten to fifteen shillings was a good order. The average was about 5s. 11d. – just the basics, potatoes, cabbage, carrots, a pound of apples. Seasons were more delineated. People made a lot of jam and bottled things. Everyone had a jam pan. Today they'd rather go to the shop and buy Tiptree; it's easier. They salted kidney beans to keep them all winter. Eggs were stored in water glass in buckets.

Eating habits were different then. I always found the poor people bought more staple foods (carrots, onions, potatoes); the better-off bought chickens, grapes and peaches. At Christmas geese were more popular than turkeys. Chickens were farm reared – they tasted different, they were thinner, Rhode Island Reds. The best table birds were reared on stubble. There was more pride among poulterers in the way they set things out and dressed them. Melons were not popular. There were more pomegranates. We got barrels of grapes in cork dust at Christmas. There was more variety of apples – Baldwins, York Imperials, and MacIntosh Reds from North America. No convenience foods. That's been the biggest change – convenience foods. The worst thing that ever happened was Clarence Bird's Eye. Kippers were smoked locally; bananas were ripened locally too. We sold some tinned things – tinned fruit – but there was no such thing as a bloody pie filling!

Food then was fresher. Everything was dirty, straight out of the ground with the roots on. We washed it – carrots and potatoes. Onions came from Spain in three-tier boxes. Apples came in barrels – a lot from Australia, Canada and New Zealand. Fish came with the head on and we filleted our own. Mackerel, herring, dover and lemon sole, salmon, haddock, cod, hake, whiting – lots of varieties of fish, and even of potatoes, all at the same time. Hull, Fleetwood and Grimsby were the main suppliers; it all comes from bloody Aberdeen now!

SOURCE 20
A London housewife

It was a London metal and plating works and I was typing invoices. I went to a Day Continuation School as well, near King's Cross. I worked hard, but I loathed it. It was boring, an awful, terrible job, typing invoices all day. I never lifted my head. Did I hate that job. Filing, typing, tea-making. I was a general dogsbody, fetching their sandwiches. I hated figures. I was so unhappy. I hated arithmetic but I used to force myself to master those figures. I never wanted to go into an office, but I had to do what my mum said. She was very dominant, mummy, and things were now so bad at home that I couldn't give up the money – I daren't leave: for the sake of five shillings a week.

A corner shop

SOURCE 21

*A London
hairdresser in a
Piccadilly store*

I started work as an 'improver', working in local shops. I had to clean windows and run errands, but my boss was a good hairdresser and he taught me well – the quicker I learnt, the more money I could make for him.

My father was a master tailor at a West End store. He put in a word for me with the manager of their salon, and after waiting for a year I moved to the West End. I had to learn new things here – deportment, good manners, the touches needed in a top salon. We used to serve the cream of people in all walks of life. You didn't have to fumble and get tongue-tied. I felt I could do it.

Fashions didn't change much. Our bread and butter was shaving. You get to know your regulars and over the years I built up a nice clientèle. A lot of the talk is small-talk – sport, hotels, restaurants, gambling, the news of the day, weather. They're not there long enough to go into deep matters. You can get too familiar. I don't call my customers by their first names – always 'Mr'. They can call me 'Sam' if they want to – that shows a good relationship between the hairdresser and his customer, but I always stick to 'Mr'. If you wanted to keep a good customer you had to keep your distance.

Questions

UNDERSTANDING

1. Why do the witnesses in Sources 16, 17 and 18 think that work was harder in those days?

2. How could a shopkeeper cheat his customers (Source 18)?

3. Why did the typist in Source 20 hate her job?

ASSESSMENT AND ANALYSIS

1. Use Sources 18 and 19 to describe how shopping and eating habits have changed since the 1920s and 1930s.

2. 'There was lots of class distinction' (Source 19). What evidence can you find of this in Sources 19 and 21?

EMPATHY

1. Show how the greengrocer in Source 19 enjoyed his work and took pride in it.

2. Would the greengrocer in Source 1 have agreed with the comments made by the farmer's daughter (Chapter 4, Source 26)?

ORAL HISTORY ASSIGNMENT

What are the main industries in your area? Collect oral evidence to show changes in working conditions in these industries.

6 The General Strike

The coal industry became the symbol of class struggle between the wars. Membership of trade unions had grown rapidly during the First World War and the miners' union, with almost a million members, was the second largest in Britain.

After 1920, however, the total membership of trade unions began to fall and the movement felt increasingly threatened. The miners led the fight to prevent cuts in wages demanded by employers, politicians and economists.

The struggle came to a head in May 1926 when the Trades Union Congress (TUC) voted to call their members out on strike in sympathetic support of the miners' refusal to accept lower wages.

The coal-mine owners, with the backing of a government inquiry, locked out those miners who rejected revised wage-rates. The Conservative government, led by Stanley Baldwin, did little to prevent the strike: they had been making preparations for such a confrontation.

The strike began on 3 May and received massive support. The unions claimed that this 'national strike' aimed only to help the miners win their industrial demands. Baldwin argued that the strike was a direct challenge to the British democratic and Parliamentary system of government.

However, the unions had made very little practical preparations and their leaders soon became frightened that a long period of strike-pay might exhaust their funds.

An Organisation for the Maintenance of Supplies used road transport to distribute food and fuel, and the more enthusiastic of the middle classes enrolled as Special Constables to help the police keep order. Violent incidents and arrests took place in many areas during the nine days of the strike.

Union leaders showed less courage than their members. Alarmed by warnings that a general strike might be ruled illegal, afraid that they might lose control, the TUC called off the strike without conditions on 12 May.

The miners felt betrayed and stayed out on strike for a further six months before they were compelled by hunger and poverty to resume work on the owners' terms.

SOURCE 1

A Church of England priest in Swindon

Welsh miners used to march up to Swindon where I was a curate, on their way to London. We put them up on the way. I often used to ask them what was the point of nationalisation. They would reply: 'The point is that there is no longer a market for raw coal. What we want is the by-products of coal – motor spirit – then Britain wouldn't be dependent on other states. Only a nationalised industry would have the money to do this, to modernise the mines.' This was invariably what they said. But they've only just recently started to make oil out of coal.

I remember one place where the railway from a mine had to go over a man's land. He was paid a royalty because the coal was transported over his land. The mine company decided to build a new line to go round him. So he claimed compensation for loss of his royalties – and he got it! He got compensation! So instead of saving money the mine finished up paying more than ever to transport the coal.

SOURCE 2

A Durham miner

The bosses were trying to increase hours for no more pay. Instead of going forward they were going back. It was the expected thing to join the union. On the whole we were more than ready to speak with one voice. Without the union we should just be as we were, with women and children in the pits.

Mounted police clear the streets at the Elephant and Castle, London

SOURCE 3

The Church of England priest from Swindon on the causes of the strike

The bosses were taking the initiative, to cut wages and extend working hours. The 1926 thing was really a lock-out. The bosses posted notices of new wage rates and said that anyone who did not accept them would no longer be employed. So it was a lock-out, not a strike.

SOURCE 4

A school caretaker from west Yorkshire, then a schoolboy

The world came to a standstill. Folks stood about. They seemed afraid to make a noise. Frightened. I've always felt sympathy for the downtrodden as the miners were then.

What point was the Government trying to make with these statistics?

SOURCE 5
A Yorkshire miner

We all came out on strike. We stuck it out, father and me, for 26 weeks. We were given some union pay until the funds were exhausted. Then father had to go for help from the Poor Law Guardians; it all had to be paid back when we started work again.

Poor Law Guardians = local officials in charge of help to the poor

SOURCE 6
A Lancashire miner

There was a miners' meeting in the pub. A greengrocer had left his barrow outside. One of the miners took a bunch of bananas under his coat and the rest followed his lead. When the greengrocer came out his cart was empty.

SOURCE 7
A mill owner who joined the Special Constables in a mining area of Yorkshire during the strike

There was no violence. The workers were happy to go back. University students and middle-class people enjoyed the strike. It was a joke with them. Miners scratched for coal on the pit heaps and sold it to make a penny or two. More people signed on as Specials than were needed. We hardly knew there was a strike. There was merely some difficulty with foodstuffs. Our way of life didn't change. It was a non-event.

Ladies organising a canteen for volunteer workers in Hyde Park, London

SOURCE 8

The Church of England priest in Swindon

In Swindon there was great sympathy for the miners. They feared that the railways might be the next for attack. Swindon was very much a family place, like a small village. There had never been anything like this before. But everyone came out in sympathy. The Strike Committee ran the town – it even vetted the news to be shown in the cinemas. If the strike had lasted longer things might have become very difficult.

SOURCE 9

The football match between strikers and Plymouth police (striped jerseys)

SOURCE 10

Stanley Baldwin, Conservative Prime Minister in 1926

(a) Extract from a broadcast on 8 May:

I am a man of peace. But I will not surrender the safety and security of the British Constitution. . . . Cannot you trust me to ensure a square deal for the parties, to secure even justice between man and man?

(b) From his speech in the House of Commons after the strike:

We should resume our work in a spirit of co-operation, putting behind us all malice and vindictiveness . . . Nor shall my sword sleep in my hand, till we have built Jerusalem, in England's green and pleasant land.

SOURCE 11

The Church of
England priest
on the aftermath
of the strike in
Swindon

When the sackings and short time came after the strike they were people I knew, my friends. We knew there was to be a big sacking. It was almost like waiting for an air raid – really rather frightening. I hardly dared to go into a house.

SOURCE 12

Six months after
the General Strike
was over, the
miners began to
return to work. A
Yorkshire miner
recalls his first
day back

When we got back to the pit the mice were starving. I don't know how they'd survived. I was sat there, eating, with my snap on my knees, and I could feel the mice nosing round my neck. Then one got on my knee and I could see my snap paper moving.

Questions

UNDERSTANDING

1. Why did the miners want nationalisation (Source 1)?

2. What is meant by 'royalty' (Source 1), 'lock-out' (Source 3), 'vetted' (Source 8) and 'constitution' (Source 10)?

3. What evidence is there in the sources that the strikers suffered hardship? What evidence is there that some of them continued to suffer when the strike was over?

ASSESSMENT

1. What, according to Sources 1, 2 and 3, were the causes of the strike?

2. Compare and contrast Sources 10 and 11.

3. The Cabinet debated whether or not to allow the football match (see Source 9) to be publicised. Why?

EMPATHY

1. Explain as a miner why you went on strike in 1926. What were your feelings at the end of the strike?

2. How would a Special Constable have justified his actions in supporting the police (see Sources 7 and 10)?

7 Life on the Dole

A world depression began in 1929 after the Wall Street crash in New York. By 1932 the total number of unemployed had risen to three million in Great Britain. The impact was most severe in the areas of the old declining industries. In some towns dependent on only one industry such as coal, cotton or shipbuilding eight out of ten workers could be jobless.

Government policies did very little to create work in these 'Special Areas'. Starvation was averted by complicated social measures. Locally financed Poor Relief, based on the workhouse, was not abolished until 1934. Almost thirteen million workers were 'insured' against unemployment in the state scheme. When entitlement to relief ran out because the workers' contributions to the fund could no longer be kept up in periods of prolonged unemployment, governments continued to pay benefit or 'the dole'.

An Unemployment Assistance Board was set up in 1934 to create a uniform, national system and to prevent extravagance. The level of benefit depended upon the total income and 'means' of a family. Local civil servants had to assess a family's needs, taking into account all savings, possessions and income. The 'means test man' was often regarded as a snooper, ready to listen to gossip and rumours of undeclared income. Families sometimes split up as younger wage-earners objected to having to support out-of-work dependents.

Unemployment hit the young, the skilled, the old and the housewife. One MP, the Earl of Portsmouth, set out to discover the social conse-quences for himself. He visited the depressed areas, wearing old clothes and allowing himself only as much money as he would have received on the dole. He ate fish and chips and drank only tea. 'I listened to street corner meetings, saw women going to work while their men watched, grey-faced and broken-hearted, from the kerb . . . I felt with them the utter dullness of their lives.'

SOURCE 1

A schoolmaster, now retired, who moved in the 1930s from the prosperous Midlands to the depressed industrial north of England

I lived in Coventry for five and a half years. It was one of the most successful communities of the 1930s. The population increased by a third in just five years. Thousands of acres were covered with new houses at £295 each. They produced bicycles, cars and machine tools. All around there was ribbon estate housing.

This was comparative affluence. People flooded in from areas of unemployment.

When I moved to Yorkshire in the late thirties I saw an enormous difference. Poverty and unemployment were so apparent.

Unemployed Man
by Percy Horton, c.*1930*

SOURCE 2
A shopkeeper in the north of England

All the mills and collieries closed. It was the only time I lost money. Prices had been very high after the First World War, then came the slump and prices fell to the bottom.

SOURCE 3
A Yorkshire mill owner

We didn't sell an ounce of anything for fourteen weeks. Father still paid the workers – five of them at a pound a week. He kept their loyalty. The rate of unemployment was 87 per cent in this area – most people were in the rag trade. There was real starvation in some families.

SOURCE 4
A mill worker in west Yorkshire

If there was a vacancy at the warehouse there would be as many as a hundred men applying for it. People were getting married on 30 shillings a week. I've seen men weep because they were out of work.

If you had a job you were a cut – an important cut – above the man in the queue. They used to 'sign on' at the Liberal Club. They were four deep all round the building. Men were just ticking over, not living.

Waiting for work – Wigan Labour Exchange, 1939

SOURCE 5

*Unemployed man,
Wigan, 1939*

SOURCE 6

*A retired
headmaster from
Lancashire, then
a schoolboy*

There was a constant stream of families on the road from Yorkshire to Lancashire. The Yorkshire people were looking for work. They stopped and asked for food and my parents were pretty generous – they usually gave them bread and cheese and a cup of tea. We used to judge a family on whether or not they offered to wash up. They were often badly clad, with no shoes.

SOURCE 7

*A builder
in Leeds*

We never knew poverty, but we were lucky. I've seen plenty of it. People on the coal heaps, scratting for coal. Even children did the same. They'd got to live somehow.

Housing was back-to-back – rubbish, definitely rubbish. There were outside toilets and terrible overcrowding. Bad houses were emptied and fumigated to get rid of bugs – bugs that looked like ladybirds. People went to the Municipal Buildings to be bathed, a damn good bath, and all their clothes fumigated. Once these things were in a house, that was it – it was something that could happen to anybody. In back-to-back houses, if they cleared one side, the bugs would get into the other side.

scratting = scratching

Collecting coal from slag heaps

SOURCE 8

Tramps were a common sight in the 1930s
(a) A Derbyshire miner

Tramps stopped at the workhouse for the night, then spent the day begging. If you gave them anything they marked your house with a white cross to encourage others to try their luck.

(b) A civil engineer in Yorkshire, then a schoolboy

Every night about 4.30 you could see tramps going to the workhouse. They weren't allowed in if they had any money, so they hid it in walls. Lads used to look for the money and pinch it. There'd be twenty a day come to the local workhouse. They never said anything to us – they sometimes threw our ball back to us, though.

SOURCE 9

A dock worker from Liverpool

The means test was the most disgraceful thing this country has ever produced. After you ran out of insurance you were means tested. You had to spend all your money, sell some of your furniture — leaving just a table, bed and necessities – and you were granted 'a reduced sum'. Potatoes, bread and gravy were the staple foods. A joint of beef cost only a shilling, but they couldn't afford it.

Tyneside in 1938. The decay of the old industries led to 'waste lands' in their 'special' areas

SOURCE 10

A watchmaker, then a schoolboy in Yorkshire

My father was on the dole. He had blisters on his feet from looking for work. He had to go into hospital once. The police called with the ambulance. According to the rules, if father went in before 12 o'clock on Wednesday night he lost seven shillings on his benefit.

We were means tested. Relief Officers came to the house to inspect us. They said, 'sell that piano, you're well off.' Anything that was good in the house they would tell you to sell it before they gave you any money. At the relief place the officials were behind wire – it might as well have been barbed wire. These fellows were happy; they treated men like dogs.

Mother sometimes had to go to the Welfare Office and beg to get us a pair of boots to go to school. These boots were stamped inside so you couldn't pawn them. There were at least five pawn-shops in this area.

SOURCE 11

A local government investigator ('means test man') in the industrial West Riding of Yorkshire

I had to take some writing tests to get this job at the Assistance Board. Then I went round visiting. It was called 'snooping'.

Lots of men didn't qualify for ordinary benefits. Once they had exhausted their ordinary claims to benefit they had to claim 'assistance'. We investigated them. I had to discover people's means, things like their savings, any children's means. There were lots of people in poverty, many who gambled and drank and left their wives without.

In one house there was an old lady living on a pension, with her daughter. In the house there was a bed downstairs, in the living room. Well, there was a big lump in the middle of this bed. So I stayed telling the tale on purpose. All at once a head popped out of the bed, the daughter's boyfriend; he couldn't stop under any longer. The old lady's allowance had to be stopped.

One woman had only two rooms and seven cats. I always carried a twist of tobacco with me to light up before I went into one of these mucky houses. But that was how she lived. A colleague visited this house and one of the cats pee'd down his ankle.

At another house there was a man standing on the kitchen table wearing nothing but a bowler hat and wellingtons, whitewashing the ceiling. The authorities had told him to do it and his attitude was that he wasn't going to ruin his clothes for *them*.

So, you can see, we got to know people really well.

Some people refused to apply till they'd lost everything. One old lass cut the laps off her husband's shirts to make knickers; the husband broke down and wept when he got the allowance. There were lots of people like that, too independent to come forward.

SOURCE 12

A Lancashire housewife

I've been to the pawn shop for other people. I wouldn't go for myself. The first time I went I cried. The fellow knew some of them so well he never looked at what was in the parcel. I saw one woman roll up with a great brass fender!

There was never any spare cash, just enough to last the week. You were always looking for your wage on Friday.

SOURCE 13

A Yorkshire shopkeeper, then a schoolboy

Dad had his photograph taken in just his working clothes. His suit had been pawned. When the photo came he was all dressed up in a best suit. The photographer had touched it up.

SOURCE 14

A Yorkshire miner

My brother-in-law was on the dole and in the Army Reserve. He used to collect coal off the muck stack, sold some and kept his own fire going. He got his milk on tick till his Reserve pay came through. Then he went to town. We were invited to his baby's christening. His Reserve pay had just come through and there was more smoked haddock there than in Grimsby docks, piles of it. Then we all went to the pub and had drinks. Then he said, 'I've got no money.' His wife said, 'You've got the milk money, haven't you?' 'Have I hell,' he said.

The Jarrow marchers halt for a meal in the Midlands in 1936 (hot corned beef and potatoes). When the marchers returned home they had their dole cut because they had not been available for work while they were marching to London

SOURCE 15

An engineer in Liverpool

Liverpool was full of Fascists, Nazis, Communists, the lot, you could take your pick. They all had different coloured shirts, they all paraded, all had their own newspapers. They were a vicious crowd. Many were unemployed, paid to march.

SOURCE 16

Sir Oswald Mosley, the fascist Blackshirt leader, reviews his followers, 1936

SOURCE 17

A greengrocer in Yorkshire

At the age of seventeen in 1937 I joined the Young Communist League. All the local lads did. A chap came round asking us to distribute leaflets against conscription, outside the Labour Exchange. I joined because we were all sheep and didn't want to conform with our Conservative parents.

SOURCE 18

An engineer from Liverpool (as Source 15)

In 1933 I went to America. My brother was already there. I went by boat and train to Detroit. Then I started from scratch again. They paid their apprentices better than our skilled workers. Living standards were far superior to here. Liverpool, where I came from, was 40 per cent slums. But American working conditions were fierce – the assembly line; we had to push the work along at a great rate; it had the same effect as the whip in earlier days. There was no holiday pay and no social security. I had five years there. They were very nice people and good towards Britain. I came back to Britain in the late thirties, when there were more jobs again.

Questions

UNDERSTANDING

1. What evidence is there in Source 1 for the affluence of Coventry?

2. What was a pawn-shop? See Sources 10, 12 and 13.

3. Explain the meanings of the terms 'dole' and 'means test' (Source 10).

ASSESSMENT AND ANALYSIS

1. What effects on people did unemployment have (Sources 7, 8, 15,1 6 and 17)?

2. What did the Liverpool engineer in Source 18 both dislike and admire about America?

3. Do you think Source 5 is a natural or a posed photograph?

EMPATHY

"They treated men like dogs.' How could the means test man in Source 11 have defended his work against such criticism?

8 The Empire: wider still and wider?

Britain's global Empire reached its greatest extent in the inter-war years. The British took their control of one quarter of the earth's land surface for granted. The Empire was part of the national consciousness.

The purpose of Empire was summarised in the phrase 'men, money, markets'. It still provided scope for British men and women as administrators, soldiers, merchants, missionaries, farmers, financiers and labourers. By the 1930s, however, immigration into Britain exceeded emigration to the Empire; many emigrants returned, homesick or disappointed. Although opportunities for investment and trade declined during the slump of the 1930s, in 1937 Britain still bought more than one third of her total imports from, and sold more than one third of her total exports to the Empire.

There was a great diversity of imperial territories. Some were self-governing dominions, such as Canada, Australia and New Zealand. Others were more directly controlled by Great Britain. There were already signs of discontent with British rule. In India, organised opposition was increasingly strong and British prime ministers wrestled with complicated schemes for granting limited measures of self-government to a continent divided by the caste system, religion and language.

Almost no one foresaw the rapid decline of Empire which followed World War Two. There was still confidence in Great Britain's imperial destiny. Many Britons still felt that, as Cecil Rhodes had said, 'To be born British is to win first prize in the lottery of life.'

Guests attending the Viceroy's garden party, New Delhi, 1938

SOURCE 1

Some reflections on the meaning of the Empire:

(a) A Yorkshire miner

We were all proud, proud to be members of the British Empire, proud to be British.

(b) A Lincolnshire housewife

Definitely we were proud of the Empire. It's the finest country in the world, they used to say.

(c) A Durham miner

Everything seemed far away. There was no news, except for the papers and the wireless. You heard very little. It meant nothing. Now and again you heard of somebody emigrating, and in a day or two they were forgotten.

(d) A hospital porter in Yorkshire, then a boy

I'd no pride in the Empire. It was never ours. It was picked and plundered. If they wanted their independence it was theirs.

(e) An accountant in Newcastle

As a schoolboy I knew of the red on the map. We thought England was a great nation. We didn't know how the people we ruled were going on. It didn't make any difference to the working man, what we were getting out of it. Who it was doing good to I don't know.

(f) A Yorkshire mill worker

I am a socialist. I was hostile to Empire at that time, hostile to intervention in any nation other than your own.

(g) A retired schoolmaster from south Yorkshire

Our science and technology had advanced standards of life; you couldn't stop it. If we hadn't done it, someone else would. And we were more civilised in our values. It was good that we should do it. The history of the British Empire will be seen as very admirable.

In villages all over Britain missionaries gave lectures on their work in the Empire. This was a prominent feature of life. The Empire was much in people's consciousness. Criticism of it was limited to intellectuals, the socially conscious, left-wing radical people.

(h) *A shopkeeper from Yorkshire, then a boy at school*

Empire Day was a big day. We waved flags. There was bunting everywhere. We were taught about the Empire at school. They showed us the red bits on the map and said: 'That's ours.' It didn't last so bloody long after that, did it? It soon fizzled out.

(i) *A railway worker from the north-east*

We were always proud. All our Empire looked to be the whole bloody world, because it was all in red. We were taught about it in history lessons. Australia – all convicts over there and that sort of thing. It was all heroes – Drake and patriotism. I don't think we exploited the Indians. Britain helped India, I'm sure we did. They've had nothing but trouble since we left.

SOURCE 2

From the Pupil's Empire Atlas, *1925*

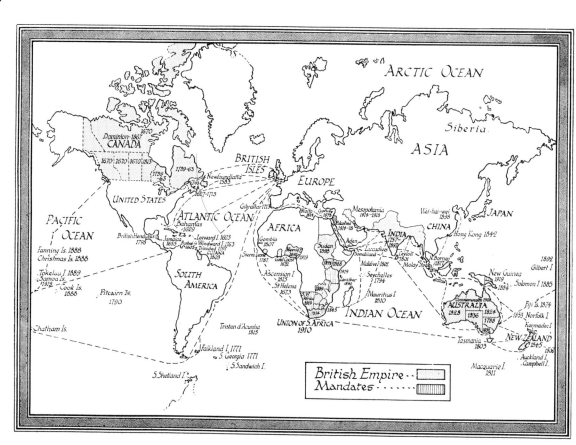

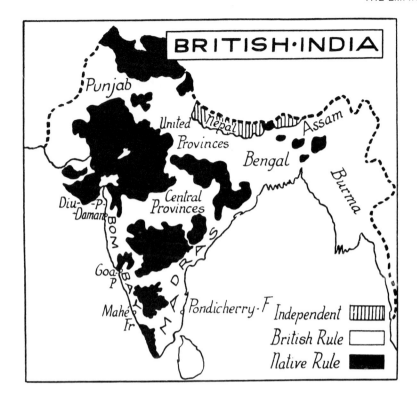

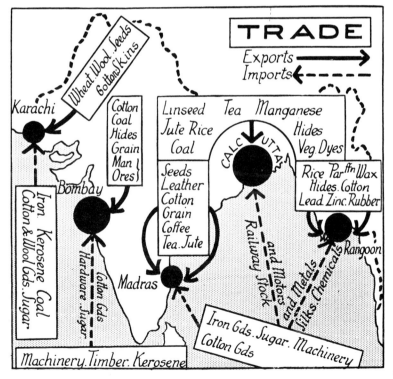

Map showing British India's major imports and exports

SOURCE 3

A farm worker from east Yorkshire who emigrated to Australia

In the 1930s Australia was in the same position as England. The depression lasted longer in Australia. The rest of the world gets over slumps three years before improvements reach there. I had come so very far and my boats were burned behind me. I was sorry that when I got there the goods were 'not as advertised', as they say. Instead of the shortage of workers in the country, as the adverts had proclaimed, there was no employment on offer. Things were in a bad way and loads of people would have returned to the UK if they'd had the price of a ticket. It might all have been a trick to unload people from England who were suffering from the depression.

SOURCE 4

A Londoner who served in the British Army in India

I joined the Army late in 1919 at the age of 14 – the Royal Engineers. I joined up because my father told me to, to get a good trade. I was seven years before going to India. On 17 March, 1926, we set out from Southampton, sailing on the *City of Marseilles* and refuelling at Port Said. Women came on there, carrying sacks of coal. Then the Suez canal for a day, the Red Sea, Indian Ocean, Bombay. At Bombay we got Tasmanian jam, a towel, and ten cigarettes. Karachi was my main posting after we'd passed through the outstations.

In 1930 I became a corporal. You needed a first-class trade, rifle and education certificates to become a corporal. Pay was twenty rupees, 30 shillings a week maximum. A corporal's pay increased by two shillings a day. We paid for our clothes and crockery. I saved enough to come home and marry in 1930.

On a typical day the barber would come and shave you at 4.30 and you got up at five in the morning. You could leave your money overnight; it was never touched. Your 'boy' would run your errands and clean your gear for a rupee a week (a boy was probably 50 years old). Boys were outcasts, untouchables, the workers, more trustworthy than any of ours. We had a good cook who always took a little black opium pill before going shopping.

At the frontier we saw the board: 'This is Afghanistan. You are forbidden to enter.' In the frontier we always carried an axe in case the Pathans attacked us. I never saw any fighting, except during the Gandhi* troubles – we faced a crowd but we didn't shoot. Gandhi tried to bring up four hundred million people from nothing. But we had more trouble from the college boys than any of the others: they caused all the troubles, easily led as Gandhiites. I have no sympathy with anybody who agitates, but Hindus living in poverty were bound to follow him. Religion, women and greed causes all wars and troubles. Agitators like Hitler and Gandhi cause trouble. When Gandhi had appendicitis he insisted on British doctors; we slipped up by making him better. I saw quite a lot of passive resistance against the British at that time.

Hindus and Sikhs could read something and repeat it word for word next day. A Mohammedan couldn't, yet he was more intelligent and able to work. They hated each other's guts. They were brought up to it, customs are different, you can't bring them together.

It's all poverty in India. Your Rajahs are rich, but there's no in-betweens, except the half-castes who run all the railways. On a railway journey you took your bed with you. You had a berth with another four. English women were locked in. There was no association with Indians; you travelled separately. The Indians would be on the bloody roof – never paid if they could help it. They used hot water from the engine to do their cooking.

The Club was for the officers. All families were confined in a compound. There was class distinction between us and the Indians and between the English as well. Officers were in a sphere of their own. We were quite contented in our own corporal's room. There were some good Indian officers – especially the Gurkhas (you could trust them with your wife, your money, your life). On Christmas Day they killed a goat and drank their white spirit.

*Mahatma Gandhi: a leader of the Indian nationalists who wanted independence from Britain.

Weather? Bloody hot! After ten o'clock in the morning we used to have to put up telephone poles with rags in our hands, they were so hot. You could grow stuff like billy-o. Hedges full of roses. We started work at six and finished at twelve. It was hard to sleep in bed because of the heat. There was this prickly heat. You ran out into the monsoons to cool down. It didn't rain then, it pissed. Each night each house lifted its shutter and got its irrigation water. In June was the chota monsoon, little rains; July to August, the big monsoon. Earthquakes were common – no birds, no sound, stillness; then your stomach goes into your throat and everyone runs outside.

I got on with Indians very well indeed, no trouble at all. One village was known as the village of thieves, and we had to pass through on our way for a holiday. There they'd take your rifle, bed, kit, clothes. We tied our rifle to our wrists, but these loose-wallahs (thieves) would use tiger grease to get it off your wrists. They'd do anything to get a rifle. We used .303 rifles which had been used all through the 1914 war. Other rifles we had which had been in use since the Mutiny.

There were snakes – small, thin ones, but one bite was enough. They were terrible things – some of them would pinch chickens. Bath houses had hornets' nests. You didn't take long over a shower in case you disturbed them. One night, turning a tap off, I was stung by an insect – they gave me two whiskies straight away.

Barracks were ancient with very solid walls, 24 to a room. They all had mosquito nets and verandahs.

If you wanted a bit of crumpet you went to the town and found a taxi driver to take you. VD was common. Women had to be of very low caste to go into brothels. In recognised brothels the women were tested every week. It cost five rupees. Not that I went, though.

In India it's all backhanders – 'backsheesh, sahib'. But then it's expected. In India time does not matter. If you said, 'I'll call tomorrow', they said, 'Kal, sahib' which meant the day after tomorrow, or never.

I once went into the Viceroy's palace. The chandelier was made in Ipswich. There's two thrones; I sat on one of them.

I thought the British were there for good. Whatever we were doing there *was* good. We did no harm. The poverty had nothing to do with us. The Indians gained from our presence. The British benefited too – gold, minerals, cotton, jute. A plane came once a week to Karachi. We could get the *News of the World* for sixpence. We could buy Cadbury's chocolate right on the frontier, and Express cigarettes at fourpence for 60. You could buy anything British.

Questions

UNDERSTANDING

1. Why was the farm worker (Source 3) disappointed with Australia?

2. Why did the Londoner (Source 4) join the army?

3. What evidence is there that the soldier in Source 4 was hostile to Gandhi?

4. Using Source 2 list five raw materials imported by Britain and five manufactures exported from Britain.

5. Why was India important to the British economy (Source 2)?

ASSESSMENT AND ANALYSIS

1. In Source 1 find two examples of people who supported the Empire, two examples of people who opposed it and one who was neutral about the Empire.

2. Compare and contrast the style and content of the remarks made about the Empire in Sources 1(g) and 1(i).

3. Can you find evidence of racial discrimination in Source 4?

EMPATHY

Write a letter from a soldier to his parents describing his life in India.

9 Leisure

The England of . . . filling stations and factories that look like exhibition buildings, of giant cinemas and dance-halls and cafes, bungalows with tiny garages, cocktail bars, Woolworths, motor coaches, wireless, hiking, factory girls looking like actresses, greyhound racing . . . swimming pools and . . . cigarette coupons.

J.B. Priestley's description shows a diversity of interests in the 1920s and 1930s. Alfred Havighurst has called it an age of 'mass civilisation'. It was still possible, as oral evidence constantly shows, to make your own entertainment in the home. At the same time radio and cinema brought more standard and uniform patterns of leisure.

Cars and coaches increased the possibilities of travel. Annual holidays, frequently but not always with pay, stimulated the growth of inexpensive British seaside resorts. The first of Butlin's holiday camps, at Skegness, opened in 1937. Hiking and youth hostelling became very popular.

Sport was more commercialised, attracting massive crowds at new stadia such as Wembley. Gambling crazes were associated with it – greyhound racing and football pools.

Following fashions was made easier by the mass production of clothes. American music – jazz and big band sounds – dominated the dance floors of the nightclubs and the 'palais de danse' of Great Britain.

SOURCE 1

*A salesman
from Cheshire*

Entertainment was not good. I acted in plays and I'm no actor. We had village comics and village pantomimes. We said, 'Aren't they good?' When we see television today we realise that they were poor. They were only good to people who had no standards by which to judge. The interval, when you sat and chatted over tea, was the best part.

SOURCE 2

*A housewife
from Lincolnshire*

Everyone made their own entertainment in those days. There was no just switching on the television. You sat round the piano or played games or just read books. Otherwise you had to go out to the pictures or the music hall.

LEN PROCTOR AND HIS HARMONICA KINGS FOR CLUB CONCERTS AND DANCES
ROCK HOUSE - 5. EIGHTLANDS ROAD - DEWSBURY

A dance band from the 1930s

SOURCE 3

*A grammar school
boy in Lancashire,
later a teacher*

Whitsuntide was the time new clothes were bought and there were Whit walks. The church Whit walk was one of the main events of the year. We went three to four miles round the country parish, singing hymns at intervals. As we passed Ada's fish and chip shop Ada threw out pennies. There was a gala in the afternoon with a brass band and games. The Roman Catholics walked the week before the Anglicans and Methodists. It was a very happy occasion. In the evening came the dance. I could guarantee I would know every one of the 150 people there.

SOURCE 4
A musician from Leicester

I played the piano and took a few pupils. Then I formed a dance band. We played all over, at dances and houses and weddings. It did fairly well.

While the band was still going I worked as a piano tuner. I went round to well-to-do houses. It took two hours to tune a piano. Some of the new-rich customers were really snooty but the traditional rich, you know, they were all right and treated me really well. I was sometimes given sandwiches.

At one house – he was a manufacturer and he had an imbecilic daughter – well, he gave me a cigar and talked about astronomy. By twelve o'clock I still hadn't seen a piano. When I'd finally tuned the piano we played a duet. I was still there at tea-time. This job followed regularly four times a year.

SOURCE 5
A London clerk

I was mad about opera and ballet from my teens. I went to the Alhambra when the Ballet Russe came. I was fascinated by the costumes, the decor and the music. It was an escape into a world of dream and fantasy. I went with friends and we sat in the gallery where it was quite cheap. I was a keen theatre goer as well.

A fashionable dance in the 1920s. What evidence of wealth can you see?

SOURCE 6
A London shop assistant

I had very little spare money, but three or four of us used to go tea-dancing every Thursday afternoon at different places. We used to pay 1s. 6d. and we had sandwiches, a pot of tea and a dance. Fantastic!

The supper-dances were much dearer. You used to ask the host to ask another guest if she wanted a dance. It was all very polite and very much a matter of courtesy. If you got a refusal it didn't matter.

SOURCE 7

*A businessman,
then a schoolboy
in Yorkshire*

It was the only pleasure we had. It was only a penny in the front seats, where you were that close to the screen you couldn't tell whether they were cowboys or Indians. You had to cheer if somebody was winning. I was so keen I got a free pass for turning the projector handle. The picture went slow when I got tired!

SOURCE 8

*The daughter of a
civil servant in
the Midlands*

Our first car was an old Renault with a wooden bonnet. I felt embarrassed by our bonnet as a child. We went to Devon to a car rally every year. My mother would never go up one particularly steep hill in the car – we children had to get out and walk with her. At the top there was a tap and a can to allow you to top up your car's water. No one dreamed of taking away the can in those days.

A proud owner. The car was a potent status symbol

SOURCE 9

*A Yorkshire
shopkeeper*

I had a car very soon. We went for runs on Sundays, picnics usually. I first looked for a car when I hadn't much money. I saw a second-hand one for a few pounds. The chap took us off for a trial run, but we didn't buy it: we had a right good run out and told him it was too expensive.

Eventually we got a car with one cylinder. If that cylinder missed it blew your hat off. I could run after my hat and leave the car running, and I could easily catch it up again.

SOURCE 10

*A Yorkshire
housewife*

Our first car was in 1932. It was a Citroën with a hood and celluloid sides. We drove that car until the mudguards dropped off – outside York Minster; we were next to a shiny Rolls Royce and I felt rather ashamed.

SOURCE 11

*A Durham
miner*

In the mines you got Whitsuntide, Easter, Christmas, all the recognised holidays. But no pay. You had to save up to guard against these periods coming on. There was never any going off anywhere.

SOURCE 12

*A greengrocer's
son in Lancashire*

We had one week's holiday a year. Father never stayed for the week. He took us there, then drove back to see to the shop. But a lot of children had no holidays and only the real aristocrats went abroad.

*A poster by A.W. Hassall. Perhaps this is why Billy Butlin
opened his first holiday camp there in 1937*

SOURCE 13

*A Scottish
accountant*

1939 was the only time the wife and I ever went abroad together, to France. We went to Paris for a fortnight and we had change out of 50 pounds. The French were delighted because we had just introduced compulsory military service.

SOURCE 14

*A Yorkshire
textile dyer*

I always liked to stop at a decent hotel. We were lucky to get a week. We always went to Whitby. In the mid-1930s Whitby was an active fishing port with about 120 boats, laden with herrings from Scotland. We went there by train. There was an orchestra on the spa. People dressed in dinner jackets. Whitby was middle class; Blackpool was working class. I preferred Whitby.

The charabanc made possible a wider variety of works' outings

SOURCE 15

*A Yorkshire
schoolmaster*

Sport was important in as much as then, much more than now, it proposed the idea of sportsmanship, a very fine thing. You hadn't the financial implications of sport. Sutcliffe and the rest *were* gentlemen. Amateurs and professionals accepted the same standards. In modern terms vandalism scarcely existed. It certainly wasn't a cult as now. Drunkards were sometimes seen in the daytime, but they used fists, not chains or razor blades.

SOURCE 16

*A Yorkshire
businessman,
then a boy*

We used to walk twelve miles to Headingley to see county cricket matches when I was a lad. We went into a greenhouse and pinched a few tomatoes and set off for the day.

Holidays at Whitby

SOURCE 17

Sandy Powell, the music-hall, radio and film entertainer from Rotherham

I never knew anything else. All I know is show business.

Early on I was a boy soprano, but when my voice broke at twelve I decided to go into comedy. I went into a juvenile spot in Newcastle, doing impersonations of George Formby and Harry Lauder. Harry Weldon was the one I liked best and as early as 1912 I made him my model. You get your favourite and model yourself on him.

My first real break came at the City Varieties in Leeds in 1918. My mother and I were doing a double turn ('Lillie and Sandy'). Wee Georgie Wood was top of the bill at the Empire in Dewsbury only a few miles away. He was off sick one night and I stood in for him. A London agent was in front and he got me two trial weeks, one in Manchester and one at the Empire in Shepherd's Bush.

In variety there was the Stoll Tour – the Colosseum in London, the Empire at Shepherd's Bush, the Hippodrome in Bristol and so on. On this tour I stayed with the same landlady in each town or city every year. I went to all these places by car, stayed at the same digs, fixed up for four years ahead, as we were booked for a five year contract. I bought a car in 1918 and I was taught to drive in Tottenham Court Road in half an hour.

The typical variety show had a pattern – an opening act to warm up the audience, such as a trick bicyclist, then a comedian with a patter, then a musical act, either solo or duet, and another speciality act to finish with.

Victor Smythe came round from the BBC to see me and asked me if I'd like to go on the radio. They liked my audition and asked me to go to London – Savoy Hill it was then, not that swanky place they have now.

I was working at the Palladium, doing the 'Lost Policeman' sketch. An agent arranged for me to do a test recording for a record company. They asked me what I would do. I said I couldn't sing, so they told me to do what

I was doing at the Palladium. They said they'd give me 60 quid for the entire copyright, or 30 pounds plus a halfpenny for every record sold. Thank God I took the royalties, thank God I did. It sold a million.

The following year I went to South Africa for three months. When I got back the recording manager came to see me. He said: 'I think I've got some good news for you.' He gave me a cheque for £175 in royalties. Then I made a contract with them and my average sales were a million a year. In those days that was a lot.

The South Africans were no different as an audience. They were all the same – if it's funny people laugh. I sometimes put in political jokes, but it was never offensive, always neutral. Whichever government was in I'd do the same joke. The thirties were years of depression, but I happened to be very lucky because my records were selling. I put a show on the radio called *Sandy Powell's Road Show,* and I was working in the theatres. I gave my first Royal Command performance in 1936 before George V. We weren't introduced to the King in those days. I did a sketch in a Royal Variety performance for George VI who was very fond of cricket, so I did a cricket sketch. I reckoned to go up and say I'd been called up for the test. Of course I meant the means test, not the bloody cricket test! Then I developed it, acting daft, saying, 'If they're all in white, how will I know which side I'm on?' and so on.

A G.E.C PRODUCT

G.E.C.
REGD. TRADE MARK

**FIDELITY
ALL-WAVE SUPERHET**
for A.C. Mains.

This latest triumph of British Radio Engineering has been tested and proved all over the world. It gives consistent reception over all distances, as distinct from spasmodic reception under good conditions, and with a quality that makes listening really worth while. Price **25 gns.**, complete with OSRAM Valves.

For full particulars and technical information write to the address below for Folder BC.7597 P, sent post-free on request.

G.E.C.
BRITISH MADE
QUALITY PRODUCTS

THE GENERAL ELECTRIC CO., LTD. *Head Office and Public Showrooms :* Magnet House, Kingsway, London, W.C.2 *Branches throughout Great Britain and in all principal markets of the world.*

The 'wireless'. The BBC was created in 1926. Advertisement from Punch, *19 August 1936*

It wasn't at all difficult to get northern humour over to southern audiences. I'm a Yorkshireman, but I don't overplay it. The real difference in north–south humour is the delivery – yes, that's it, the delivery.

The period of the dole was personally my best one. I went on with my little show and made it a real family one. I was playing at the Empire in Nottingham when the Jarrow marchers came through. I gave them 200 tickets and invited them to see the show. They were a glorious audience.

The best audience I ever played before was in Maidstone gaol. We had murderers and Leopold Harris the fire-raiser there. The warder said to me, 'We've got all the best criminals in here, you know.' There was one murderer who'd joined in the hunt for the child he'd murdered. He played the saxophone and drums. He seemed a hell of a nice fellow. I also played at Wormwood Scrubs and they were a very nice audience – a captive audience.

The worst audience was at the Glasgow Empire. They didn't like English comedians at all. I got worse than the bird – deathly silence. It's a horrible feeling. I don't know why they did it. It was anti-English. They loved American and coloured acts, but not English. But I went back. It was part of my route. You couldn't refuse. It was part of the contract. Friday night, first house was the worst: they hated English comedians and they just wouldn't laugh. Yet at the Pavilion, just around the corner, they were a great audience. It was just the tradition of the Glasgow Empire.

Tooting cinema. Going to the pictures became almost a religion

I did six or seven films too, before the war started. At first they were little five minute things for Pathé Pictorial, then longer ones for British Lion.

I had plenty of mistakes and embarrassing moments. That's how my catch phrase, 'Can you hear me, mother?' started. We were doing a sketch round the microphone on the radio, and I dropped my script, so I had to fill in time. So I said it two or three times: 'Can you hear me, mother?' It was just a line in the script from a sketch called 'Sandy at the North Pole', but it caught on and kept on, thank God. In the show business game you've got to be ready for anything. If someone was off you went on.

I remember right at the beginning of this period, on Armistice Day, 1918. I was playing at the Hippodrome, Devonport. I should have joined up that very day. They sent a telegram to my agent: 'Powell need not attend.' If peace hadn't come just then it might have been different. I might have missed all that luck.

Sandy Powell and his wife, Kay. 'Can you hear me, mother?'

Ford V·8

To or from the swimming-pool there's only one way to travel " de luxe," in the luxury-car for the economically-inclined, the FORD V-8, that does so much, so easily, so well, *and* so inexpensively ! The Local Ford Dealer invites you to know all about it, perhaps for the first time realising how very little this beautiful car costs, to buy, insure, run, and maintain always at its best. Literature on Request : All Prices at Works : Dealers Everywhere.

Ford V-8 Cabriolet illustrated, **£240** *(£22 . 10s. Tax)*
Alternative Body-Styles from £230.

FORD MOTOR COMPANY LIMITED, DAGENHAM, ESSEX. LONDON SHOWROOMS   88 REGENT ST., W.1

Advertisement from Punch, *10 June 1936*

Questions

UNDERSTANDING

1. How did people 'make their own entertainment' in this period? (Sources 1 to 4).

2. Why did the London clerk (Source 5) love opera and ballet?

3. Why did Sources 8, 9 and 10 feel embarrassed about their cars?

4. Why did the miner in Source 11 have to 'guard against' holidays?

5. What different holiday experiences are described in Sources 11 to 14?

6. How did Sandy Powell get into show business? (Source 17).

ASSESSMENT AND ANALYSIS

1. How has television changed habits of leisure?

2. Explain why 'financial implications' may conflict and clash with 'the idea of sportsmanship' (Source 15).

3. Explain why Sandy Powell considered the period of the dole his 'lucky time' (Source 17).

EMPATHY

1. Use the evidence in Source 17 to make up a brief review of a typical variety show in this period.

2. What aspects of Sandy Powell's life would you have liked and disliked?

ORAL HISTORY ASSIGNMENTS

1.   **BODYLINE!**
         In our opinion bodyline bowling is unsportsmanlike. Unless stopped at once it is likely to upset the friendly relations existing between Australia and England. (Telegram of 18 January, 1933 from the Australian Cricketing Board of Control to the MCC)

In the 1930s there was a cricketing controversy between England and Australia over 'bodyline' bowling. Try to interview people who can remember the episode. What was the dispute about? Find out the names of the cricketers involved. What are the attitudes of people towards them now? What does this exercise tell you about the difficulty of distinguishing between 'fact' and 'opinion'?

2.   Choose one specific type of leisure activity and organise an oral investigation into its origins and development.

10 Collecting Oral Evidence

There is no one 'right' way of collecting and using oral evidence. This section simply offers some practical hints.

1. Choosing the period and topics for investigation.

There has been a wide variety of oral history projects. Some are very narrow and drily academic (for example, interviews with civil servants about the making of educational policies); most oral history has been local – studies of a small area over a relatively short period. Local history is the easiest way to begin oral studies because the material is readily available.

Obviously you have to choose a period within living memory, for which it will be easy to find people to interview. But remember that someone who was born after 1900 might still be able to recall his or her grandparents' memories of the mid-nineteenth century: such second-hand memories are also worth recording because they are otherwise in danger of being lost.

You should not expect to learn all your history from the people you interview. The project should be carefully researched before the interviews begin. It is essential to know the background and to have plenty of good ideas for questions. Old people often forget precise dates – the general strike, the year of the abdication, the date of an explosion in a local coal mine –

and need some help or prompting to get their bearings in the past.

2. Preparing a questionnaire and conducting the interview.

A good questionnaire is the key to a good interview. Drawing up a set of questions will help you to clarify your own ideas of what you are trying to discover. You should begin with easier factual questions (such as date and place of birth) before moving on to more difficult questions about opinions and beliefs. In the light of the experience of one or two interviews, the questionnaire can be amended and improved. (Some sample questions are given at the end of the section.)

It is a good idea to talk informally to the interviewee for a while before turning to the formal questionnaire. You should not keep rigidly to the questions you have prepared in advance; often the most interesting conversations are those which wander from the original point. Interviews should not last too long – anything over an hour can be tiring for the speaker and interviewer.

3. Equipment.

Ideally interviews should be recorded on a cassette recorder, with an external microphone placed on a table between the speaker and interviewer. A C90 cassette is the best length: be ready to stop the conversation while you change sides!

Be prepared to make a written record of the interview if the machinery should fail. The batteries might run down, or the electrical sockets may be the wrong type, or the speaker might refuse to be recorded. You should make some written notes in any event, listing the order in which topics have been discussed, to make it easier to locate the parts of the tape you found most useful. It is probably best to have two people to conduct the interview, one to ask questions and one to make notes and keep an eye on the cassette recorder.

4.   Finding subjects for interview.

At first it is probably best to interview members of your family or family friends, even if this is only practice for more ambitious projects. They will be able to direct you to other contacts. Old peoples' homes and charities often welcome young people involved in historical projects and local history societies can provide help.

5.   Recording the results.

The interviews should be transcribed into written form and reduced to a manageable length. Irrelevant, hesitant, boring or confused passages can be cut out at this stage, but the original wording, including dialect or slang, should be retained.

Witnesses sometimes produce other forms of evidence – photographs, or documents such as old wage slips, or wartime souvenirs. Copies or photographs of these can enhance your project.

The final task is to report your findings. This can take many forms – for example, an essay, an exhibition, a talk or a cassette in the style of a radio programme using extracts from the interviews.

Some sample questions on the period 1918–1939

The end of the First World War

What did you do on Armistice day, 1918? Did you support the war? Why? How did the war affect your life, members of your family, friends?

Motherhood

Did you have children? How many? Where – home or hospital? Did you give up work to have a child? What advice did you have? Breast feeding? Financial hardships in having children? Clothes, pram, cot, toys, christening?

Childhood and school

What are your first memories of childhood? Parents – were they strict? Did you ever disobey them? How did you amuse yourself? Did you enjoy school? What type of school did you go to? Facilities (compare with modern schools)? What subjects? Do you remember particular teachers, favourite subjects, games?

Work

Where did you work? What did you do? How did you travel to work? At what time did you begin? How many hours per day, per week? Holidays? Describe a typical day at work. Did the work change during this period (for example, new machinery)? Did you get on well with other workers, employer? Did you belong to a trade union? Did it do anything for you? Did you ever take part in a strike (the General Strike)? What wages did you receive? Did you need any qualifications? Were there dangers in the work? Were you ever unemployed? Dole? Means test? Poor Law – workhouse? Did any of these affect you, your family, neighbours, friends? Did your standard of living change in these years – car, holidays, better conditions? Was promotion possible, frequent? What did you most enjoy/dislike about your work?

Index